THE MID CAREER ACTION GUIDE

A PRACTICAL GUIDE TO MID CAREER CHANGE

Second Edition

DEREK KEMP • FRED KEMP

KOGAN
PAGE

First published in 1991
Second edition 1992

Kogan Page Limited
120 Pentonville Road
London N1 9JN

© Derek Kemp and Fred Kemp 1991, 1992

British Library Cataloguing in Publication Data

A CIP record for this book is available from the British Library.

ISBN 0-7494-0869-3

Typeset by DP Photosetting, Aylesbury, Bucks
Printed and bound in Great Britain by
Biddles Limited, Guildford and King's Lynn

Contents

Acknowledgements

This guide would have been incomplete but for the cooperation received from those we consulted in various professions.

We must record our special thanks to Bernard Buttle, our former co-author, who gave generously of his time and expert advice, and Howard Ling for his invaluable guidance.

Where specialist knowledge was necessary, we consulted experts. Charles Johnson, a professional psychologist from PRD of St Albans helped to compile Chapter 1. Simon Burke of Arctic Life & Pensions of Bramley, Guildford generously allowed us to condense the paper he prepared on pensions. The staff of Resources Limited of Gerrards Cross assisted with the drafting of the exercises reproduced in Chapter 5.

Questionnaires were returned and contributions received from employers and professional associations. We are indebted to Mrs J Barraclough, Senior Personnel Officer, British Gas; Miss J M Harding, Recruitment Adviser to Boots the Chemists; Jennifer Goddard, Careers Promotion Officer of the Law Society; Peter Broadbent, Registrar, the Landscape Institute; Jonathan Parkins, Assistant Director, Education and Training, Institute of the Motor Industry; Margaret Catran, Director, Professional Standards, Royal Town Planning Institute; Catherine Byrne, Careers Officer, Chartered Association of Certified Accountants; J W Roskill of the Association of British Dispensing Opticians.

In our search for practical information, we met people from many walks of life in order to draw upon their collective experience. In particular, we must thank the following for their assistance: Sue Cornford, Catherine Prest, Dawn Roach, Carole Simpson, David Jones, Peter Mirfin, Lucy Pimblett, Janette Cotton, Madeleine Mansell, Siobhan Connolly, Pat Barlow, Alex Sharman, Tim Walby and Barry Walker.

Chapter 1
The Mid-Career People

Who are the mid-career people? This question is not as simple as it seems, but then questions about people never are. You can be classed as being in mid-career because of your age, because of your work experience, or because of your non-work related experience. No two people have the same mix of skills, ambitions and experience, so real career counselling has to be carried out on an individual basis. There are some basic categories and types, but no individual can be pigeon-holed precisely.

Nevertheless, we will make some generalisations about people in mid-career, not because individuals necessarily have much in common, but because there are a great many myths and misconceptions which need to be dispelled. This is particularly true in the case of more mature workers who are the subject of some misguided and unfortunate stereotyping. It is a great pity if you come to believe that these stereotypes, myths and misconceptions apply to you.

There are four main types of mid-career people:

1. Those who are currently in work but who want a change of career.
2. Those who have been put out of work and did not want to be.
3. Those who have left by choice and now want to return.
4. Those in their thirties or older with little or no work experience who are trying to start a career.

We will briefly consider each of these types.

1. Those seeking change

You can be in this group for a variety of reasons and how you feel about yourself will differ markedly, depending on the reasons. Some of you will be looking for a change simply because you are bored with what you are doing; others will be looking for new challenges; some people will be looking for better promotion or development opportunities; others will have had enough of working for other people and be looking for an opportunity to strike out on their own.

If you are in this group, the important characteristic is that you are currently using your work skills. You are used to the routine and pressures of work. Work itself should not hold any fears. Changing jobs is, however, a stressful experience. Among the threats facing you if you change jobs are the potential loss of job security and the fear that you may not have the skills required for other jobs. Of course, this may be true.

To change jobs you may need to gain new skills or to update old ones. You may feel that the skills you have are outmoded. The training effort required may be daunting. A change can be risky. Similarly, any loss of income can harm your personal and social life as well as your financial situation.

But not all career changes need to be like this. The more closely the new occupation resembles a previous job, the easier it will be to transfer your existing skills. This does not mean that you must choose the same occupation. Instead, you need to consider whether the new job uses your existing skills, even if it uses them in new ways. There will, of course, be fresh relationships to form and perhaps a surprising range of facts to learn, but as long as you are confident in your existing skills the new job will be that much easier to master.

2. Those reluctantly out of work

If you have lost your job, in one way or another, you will be in this group. Obviously, there is a clear distinction between being sacked and being declared redundant, but there are also some important distinctions to be drawn between the different ways in which individuals can come to be dismissed through redundancy. The personal significance of being one of a group of workers whose services are no longer required is very different from that of being on the workforce of a company which has gone into liquidation. The latter is much less likely to have an adverse effect on your self-confidence or confidence in your skills but, in fact, you may well feel as bad as someone who has been sacked.

You probably still possess well-developed and practised work skills and have your work habits intact. But there are some critical differences: you are likely to be upset or angry or emotionally distressed. Your self-confidence may have taken a knock, especially if other workers have been retained by the company.

Perhaps most important, you are likely to be unprepared for the task of looking for new work. You may not have begun to consider what skills you have and where and how you can market those skills. You may be unwilling to consider new types of work, even if you were dissatisfied in your previous job.

If you have been out of work for some time you will start to worry about the deterioration of your skills. You will be concerned about your ability to get back into the work routine and whether there is any work for which you are really suited. Worse, you may feel you are staring poverty in the face. You could also have experienced several rejections from job applications which further dent your self-esteem. You may feel your age is against you. The crucial issue for this group is how you can best be helped to help yourself. It is not easy to remain optimistic in the face of disappointment, or to keep in perspective the skills you have to offer.

3. Those returning to work

The majority of our third group are likely to be mothers considering the possibility of a return to paid employment. But you may have taken early retirement or voluntary redundancy and since thought better of it. Again, how you feel about returning to work will depend to a large extent on how long it is since you last worked. It also depends on how much you enjoyed working in the first place.

Unfortunately, most people in this group lack confidence about returning to work. You may believe that your work skills have evaporated. You may be aware of the change that will result in your lifestyle and of the effort involved. Running a home may be an exacting task, but the skills needed at home are different from those needed at work and the apparent gap can be intimidating. You are in good company. A survey found that 85 per cent of women with children were interested in returning to work at some stage.

4. Late starters

This group also is made up largely but not exclusively of women. Most will be women who married or had children young, either before going into employment or before having had the time to develop a career. Others will never have had to work before – perhaps because of a long-standing illness or failure to find work.

If you are in this category none of you will have developed work habits, even though you may have developed habits of self-organisation that are very similar. For example, organising fund-raising events, such as school fairs, requires skills which are much in demand.

The worry for many in this group is fear of the unknown. You ask:

'Am I too late starting work?'
'Am I capable of learning new skills now?'
'Will I be able to fit in?'

The answer to these questions is to consider what you have to offer as objectively as possible and to aim at realistic targets.

Conclusion

A common thread here is the fear of not being able to cope with a new job. This is partly anxiety about change and partly worries about the effects of ageing. But these fears are misconceived.

What are the common, but erroneous, stereotypes of the mature worker? Older workers are often thought to be:

slower in their performance
less capable
less efficient
less productive
less competent
less able to learn new skills
more accident prone
more rigid in their attitude
more resistant to supervision
more irritable
less healthy.

In fact, only one of these statements has been found to be true. There is no escaping it – we all get somewhat slower as we get older, and we have less energy. We all tend to move more slowly, recover from illnesses more slowly and, to a lesser extent, think more slowly. Even here there is an exception – speech does not become slower with age.

There are, however, any number of ways in which the more mature compensate for being slower. If you are in this group you tend to be steadier and more reliable. You are at least as accurate – some have suggested more accurate – in the work you do. You tend to be more motivated and enthusiastic about work, more tolerant of management controls, to take greater pride in what you produce, and to have better work habits. Of course, you may be motivated by different things.

Typically, there is greater concern for security, both financial and personal, but it is associated with greater self-awareness and more realistic expectations of career prospects. You may not have the driving ambition of the young but you tend to be more self-confident and have a better idea of what you are aiming for.

The net effect is that the mid-career changer can be just as productive as the younger worker. Indeed, at least one researcher has claimed that total work output is highest for workers in their fifties. You are much more likely actually to be *at work*. Absenteeism is lower and you are less accident prone, although recovery from injury usually takes longer. You change jobs less frequently, partly because of increased concern with security. Although heart problems are more common, respiratory problems are less frequent and your mental health tends to be better. Young people are every bit as liable to 'burn out' as older ones. Hearing and sight also remain good, at least until about the age of 55. All in all, you are a better bet for employers than is your younger counterpart.

The advantages of the mature worker also apply in the area of training and learning new skills. Mature students typically are keen to learn and can learn just as much as younger ones, though they may respond better to different training methods. In particular, the pace of learning may need to be different. Part of the underlying notion that more mature people are less able to learn new skills is based on another faulty assumption, namely that intellectual ability diminishes from about the age of 30.

The major skill which is thought to decline is the ability to solve problems. This was a common belief for many years. Not long ago one researcher in this field said, 'in his late thirties and forties, a man falls well below his peak levels of functioning'. It is now known that there is no noticeable decrease in intellectual ability until well after reaching the sixties. Any slight changes can be offset by the use of various compensatory strategies, such as memory aids, or by bringing to bear greater experience or, indeed, by getting a little of the right sort of training and encouragement.

There is one final, crucial point to keep in mind. The variation in performance is much greater among older workers than it is among the young. If you think of yourself as among 'the more mature group of workers' you must remember that this variability is related to your perception of yourself. As the saying goes, you are only as old as you feel.

If you think of yourself as past your best, and believe in the stereotypes of older people, that is how you will perform. You don't have to believe it!

Case study: The Brigadier

One person who did not believe it was the Brigadier. He talked about his last months of service in the Army. At 54 he was nearing the retirement age, but he decided to act in advance of the formal date for three compelling reasons: his wife's state of health, the conclusion that further promotion to Major-General was unlikely, and lack of money. This decision was not an easy one. Initial thoughts of a quiet job in the country had to be discarded because his gratuity, paid when leaving the services, would barely cover the deposit on a house.

Having informed the Ministry of Defence of his intentions, he started to look around for suitable employment. He first visited one of the companies offering career analysis and went through the usual psychometric tests. The suggestions of a career in music or working in the environmental field were not really practicable. A poorly paid job was not his target, and opportunities in the environmental scene are more for young science graduates than for management. The Officers' Association was more helpful. Its lectures were good, useful contacts were made, and suggestions included the voluntary sector/fund raising. The Brigadier also attended a practical course on bursarship sponsored by the Joint Services Resettlement Advice Office. It covered financial management and information technology, with one session presented by a bursar from a boys' school. An unsuccessful job application was made for a bursar post at an Oxford college, but the Brigadier's enthusiasm waned as he began to appreciate the rather limited role and salary of a bursar. Companies selling financial services were persuasive, but that idea did not appeal to him.

Then the Officers' Association forwarded an advertisement for the post of Chief Executive (CE) to a large local authority. He submitted his CV and at an interview with the recruitment consultant learned that the authority was to undergo a reorganisation. Of the 16 applicants the Brigadier was one of only five called for second interview. The others all had local authority experience. As part of the selection procedure the candidates were given an actual project to study overnight. It concerned a legal problem regarding a newly constructed car park. With his years of experience in dealing with similar exercises in logic the Brigadier did not find it difficult. He was offered the appointment and gladly accepted it. Within six weeks of taking office he had prepared a corporate strategy for the council. It defined the council's objectives, placed them in order of priority, and provided the basis of a draft ten-year plan. His plans were accepted.

The Brigadier believes that his 35 years' experience in the Army has served him well. Based on this he made a point of meeting everyone on the council payroll. This had seldom happened before. Senior management morale was restored when they were given complete responsibility for their staff. Furthermore, the Brigadier would not tolerate backdoor outflanking approaches to the CE via councillors. He always consulted his top officials before every policy move and made a point of taking their advice.

When asked what he would say to others leaving the forces in similar circumstances he replied: 'There are pitfalls for the ex-serviceman and woman. You must accept the political side of life in civilian organisations. There will be conflicts of interest. You must be seen to be consistent and fair to everyone. Stick to broad objectives and be direct, open and honest in all your dealings. I have found that military training and Staff College have developed the power of logic and the ability to see the wood for the trees.

'One significant difference will be noticed. Service people enjoy public esteem, but the public's attitude to a council can be antagonistic – this can hurt and you must have a good sense of humour. I find holding this post a stimulating experience and one which I am well equipped to deal with, thanks to my service background.'

The Brigadier's experience is an excellent example of a mid-career person making a successful transition from one career to another. You can also see that his approach to the career change was, to a very great extent, based on his previous experience. All successful mid-career changers must be able to build upon the legacy of their past experience.

Chapter 2
The Mid-Career Change Process

No job change is easy but the opportunities are there. This guide is intended to maximise your chances of a successful and smooth transition to a more satisfying career. We start by considering the environment in which you will be making your decisions.

The employment prospects for all age groups will be transformed in the 1990s in a way which can only be described as 'revolutionary'. The fact that this is going to occur is of some academic interest, but who it will affect and by how much you can benefit or lose is now up to you. The reasons for such changes are never simple, but in broad terms the post-war 'baby boom' is over and the effects of this on the job market are beginning to be felt.

This shortfall is further compounded by two factors: first, employers will not just be competing for young employees with other companies and organisations. The largest competitors will be the further education establishments – schools, colleges, polytechnics and universities.

Second, international competition for young people, especially the better qualified, will also increase. The low levels of pay in the UK compared with Europe make this country an excellent target for recruiters from the Continent. The demographic changes in some countries in Europe are even more dramatic than in Britain – the import of skilled, independent young labour will be essential. The next area of interest is obviously how British companies will react to this predicament. The first and most short-term solution is bound to be an increase in the salaries offered to young people by those employers who can most easily afford to 'buy' staff.

The policy of increasing salaries – for all staff if they are to be retained and differentials maintained – will be both expensive and inefficient as a means of keeping staff unless organisations consider other changes as well. This will lead inevitably to the introduction of relatively new employment policies aimed at retaining staff and recruiting new personnel. Often they will be seeking to attract staff from new sources; for example, women returners, more mature workers who are considering a change of career, disabled people. So where does this leave you?

There are more opportunities and far more scope for achieving a

Figure 2.1 *The mid-career change process*

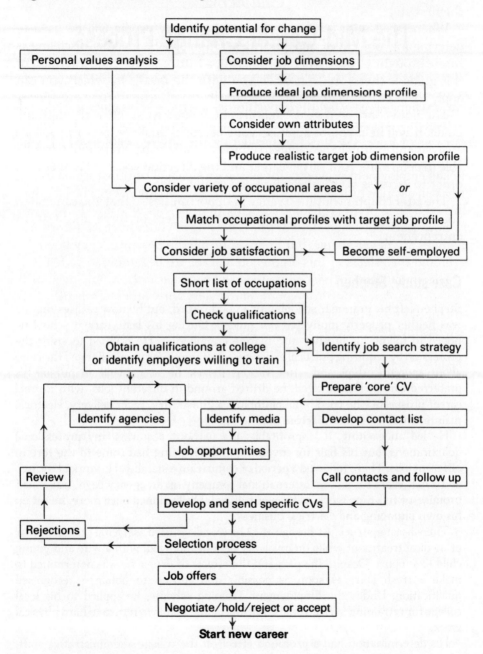

well-paid and satisfying career than ever before. Your difficulty is in taking the first step.

When faced with a new work situation many people will be used to determining objectives and priorities rationally. Sadly, this discipline is rarely brought to bear when considering a future career. The intention of this guide is therefore to provide you with the means by which you can apply these work-related skills to yourself.

The flow-chart on page 17 indicates how you can progress through the guide. It will help you to appraise your personal qualities, perform a skills analysis and examine the values to which you subscribe. You should then be able to determine your target career and the direction you need to follow in order to increase your satisfaction and contentment.

The later chapters outline a range of opportunities so that you can match your requirements with various potential careers or forge ahead as an entrepreneur.

Case study: Stephen

Stephen left his grammar school with a good record, but he now realises that he was neither properly motivated nor guided. During his last years at school he hoped to follow his brother into marine engineering. He planned to enter the profession by acquiring practical experience, but the government changed the rules about apprenticeships and, after various delays, he was unable to pursue his preferred career. Discouraged, he drifted around in different jobs, with no real career prospects – he tried retail plumbing, a gunsmith's, yacht delivery, electrical maintenance, jeans manufacture, and so on.

He led an exciting, if unprofitable, life without acquiring any professional qualifications, but his flair for inventing and designing had come to the fore in different jobs. There followed a period of comparative stability. He worked for two and a half years for a large international company on an agency basis, but a 'half promise' of full-time work was never fulfilled. Disillusioned once more, he set up his own plumbing and electrical business.

Then disaster struck. At the age of 43 he was diagnosed as having cancer. A year of medical treatment while on invalidity benefit followed, with a wife and young child to support. Despite the pain and the effects of drugs, he was determined to make a fresh start as soon as possible and retrain to obtain a recognised qualification. Under the Employment Training scheme, he applied to his local college for retraining in electronic servicing, being unable to return to hard physical work.

His determination had a profound effect on the college's administrative staff, who placed him on their one-day-a-week City and Guilds' course. Equally important, they secured a placement for him with an electronics company where he could gain practical experience. He not only overcame the effects of pain-killing drugs, managing to attend both college and work, but was also upgraded to the second year of the C & G course.

Stephen's employers were delighted when he designed a device for opening the cases of personal stereos easily and without damage, and a gauge for measuring belts. Soon he was nominated for an award and invited to a 'European Service Expo' in Brussels where he received a prize in recognition of his inventiveness. He is now working full time at the electronics company and looks forward to a promising career.

Today Stephen says: 'If you are willing to retrain, the opportunities are there for anyone. You have to show people that you can do it. Get your foot in the door. Meet people face to face who can help and, most of all, show your enthusiasm. Only then can you start to make progress.'

Many career changes are far less dramatic than Stephen's, but what he managed, with all his disadvantages, illustrates what you can achieve with courage and determination.

Chapter 3
Future Potential

Before embarking on what might be a totally new direction, it is always wise to know the general levels of growth or decline expected in that area. New employment projections up to the year 2000 can give some useful insights (see Figure 3.1) but always remember that they can be subject to wide margins of error when changes in the economy or the political arena undermine their basic assumptions.

Most projections estimate that there will be continued growth in employment opportunities towards the year 2000. Without exception, the estimates suggest that the largest percentage growth will occur in the service sector. The service sector includes tourism and leisure – hotels and catering and miscellaneous services – which account for almost three-quarters of the projected growth. This area includes both those in employment and the growth associated with those in self-employment. There is some disagreement about the rate at which business services will grow, but again there is no disagreement that this will be an area of relatively rapid expansion.

At the other end of the scale, manufacturing employment is expected to fall because of increased competition, increased productivity and the use of new technology. In looking at opportunities in the range of occupations, growth is expected in almost all categories. Most of these are expected to be in the managerial, administrative and professional classifications. Clerical and secretarial employment is still expected to grow in terms of numbers of jobs, although its share of the overall market is falling because of the increasing use of new technology. The growth in opportunities for craft and skilled manual work will continue as demand from the construction industry offsets the decline for similar trades in manufacturing. The one area where growth is not expected is in operatives and labourers. Here a small decrease is forecast. The greatest increase within the professional section, which is in itself the area of most rapid growth, is in the sphere of health and welfare and business services.

The main current skill shortage areas are:

Teachers (in specific subjects)

Information technology professionals
Machinists
Welders
Builders
Carpenters
Plasterers
Professional engineers (electrical/electronic, instrument, mechanical, production)
Managerial staff.

Figure 3.1 *Projected employment change by industry group, UK*

	Employment change 1988–2000 %	Average annual growth %
Agriculture	−11	−1.0
Mining, etc	−23	−2.2
Utilities	−21	−2.0
Metals, minerals, etc	−9	−0.8
Chemicals	+4	+0.4
Engineering	−10	−0.8
of which		
Mechanical engineering	−18	−1.6
Electrical engineering	−11	+0.9
Motor vehicles	0	0.0
Food, drink and tobacco	−20	−1.8
Textiles and clothing	−23	−2.2
Other manufacturing	−1	−0.1
Construction	+14	+1.1
Distribution, etc	+9	+0.7
of which		
Distribution	+5	+0.4
Hotels and catering	+20	+1.5
Transport and communication	+12	+0.9
Business services	+15	+1.1
Miscellaneous services	+55	+3.7
Health and education	+10	+0.8
Public administration	+3	+0.2
Whole Economy	**+8.6**	**+0.7**

Employers' changing attitudes and approach have affected their recruitment methods, payment levels and benefit packages, working environments and career planning strategies. The approach taken by mid-career changers is also altering.

Broadly speaking, they rank their priorities in the following order:

1. The job itself – what level of interest and satisfaction does it contain?
2. Details of the 'package' including promotion prospects, pay and benefits, working environment and job security.
3. The company's reputation, location and image.

Further education

Further education is an option available to every adult in the UK. With skill shortages in mind, you should consider it if you are contemplating a significant career change. Perhaps your new employer will pay for you to receive further education and training. More commonly, however, you will have to make the investment in time and money. The forms of study can range from distance learning (which can be carried out at home and is becoming popular) to attendance at polytechnics, colleges of further education and universities. We will deal with these in more detail in Chapter 7, after you have analysed your objectives and aims in greater detail.

Further education is not something to be ruled out because of age. Quite the reverse – it is obvious that mature students are going to be in the majority on many courses in the near future.

Small businesses and self-employment

When considering your future, you would be well advised not to ignore the possibility of becoming self-employed or, for the more ambitious, starting your own small business.

During the 1980s there was a significant growth in the number of small businesses registered for VAT. At the start of 1980 there were 1.29 million and this rose to 1.57 million by the start of 1989 – representing a net increase of over a quarter of a million or 22 per cent. What is even more important is that the rate of increase accelerated towards the end of the 1980s.

Therefore this is another mid-career option you may wish to bear in mind. In Chapter 9 we consider the alternative forms of enterprise.

Case study: Pat

Pat graduated in foreign languages and promptly joined the aero-engine industry. Her next move was to work on chemical plant construction contracts in the eastern bloc. This experience honed her negotiating skills – both as a buyer and a seller.

At the age of 25 she became a commercial and industrial vehicle buyer as well as a negotiator of supply contracts for the North Sea oil industry. A year later she moved to a company in the BOC group as senior buyer and later became the head of purchasing for a manufacturing division.

Pat is now a senior member of the Institute of Purchasing and Supply (IPS) and on several committees dealing with contracts management and training. At the age of 34 Pat joined KPMG Peat Marwick McLintock. She now lectures on negotiating, drawing on her varied experience in the UK and Europe, and is an informed speaker on the Single European Market, as well as advising clients on purchasing and contracts at national and international level.

Recently she has been involved in work in the transport industry for the European Commission concerning new legislation and has advised the UK electricity and water industries on European procurement law. She has also assisted government departments in formulating counter-proposals to EC procurement rules.

Pat has therefore worked for five employers gaining experience in five distinct areas: contracts, procurement, EC law, manufacturing, transport.

Each move broadened her experience, and her knowledge of languages opened doors which would have remained shut to many.

Pat's comment was: 'You have much more potential and ability than you think. It is important to recognise and seize opportunities as they arise. In that way you stretch yourself and acquire new skills.'

Every step Pat took was clearly well considered. Plan your future in a similar way, taking into account every possible option and ensuring that your final decision is realistic. That is not to say that a good idea, or a new approach to an old problem, will not be successful.

Chapter 4
Why Change?

Since the start of this book we have asked you to consider the following:

First, the environment for change – identifying the ever increasing opportunities and the possibility of changing your job and/or career.

Second, in general terms, who and what you are. The aim is for you to be able to identify yourself at some point along the developmental scale of maturity.

In this chapter and the next you will be giving consideration to the possibility of change. Is a change necessary? What change should be made? Why do you want to change? To make the correct decision it is advisable to be clear in your answers to all these questions. In some cases, you may feel certain that you already have the answers. Your job may just have been made redundant or your family may have moved recently, but nevertheless we strongly advise you to read these chapters carefully. Change is an opportunity and to obtain maximum benefit we should now examine some basic considerations.

Some have change thrust upon them but for all those initiating change the overall aim is to increase their level of satisfaction. Alternatively, if you have little option but to change, the aim will normally be to minimise any loss of satisfaction or to turn the situation to your advantage. Broadly speaking, there are 13 indicators and we will consider them in random order.

1. The outgoing individual

That happiness, optimism and an outgoing disposition are the traits of those most satisfied with life is to be expected. More important, those who can be so described rarely consider that they feel seriously depressed or discontented at any stage of their adult lives. By the time people with a high level of satisfaction are in their forties or fifties, there is a huge difference between them and those who are less well satisfied, which may be explainable only in terms of bio-chemistry.

Perhaps the main issue here is the capacity to project a positive attitude.

2. Outside commitment

This refers to the ability to find meaning in work, and in other people, with some social aim. Success in this area provides the recipients with both direction and meaning to their lives.

3. Positive attitude to failure

Highly satisfied individuals still suffer failures. The difference lies in the fact that in their own self-appraisal they are far less likely to record these occurrences as 'failures'. Their attitude is to see them as positive opportunities from which they have often benefited in the longer term.

4. Overcoming adversity

People who display the highest level of satisfaction often report having had to overcome more adversity than others. They appear to face each crisis as a challenge and overcome it with more creative solutions and a more resourceful approach than do many others. They tend to make things happen rather than have things happen to them by chance. The most satisfied people appear to spend little time on being introspective. They look forward all the time, only becoming concerned with self-analysis when faced with a major challenge.

5. Success within most western cultures

There are three main areas in which almost all individuals look for success: family security, a sense of attainment and material well-being. Not surprisingly, those people showing the highest level of satisfaction feel that they have attained all three of these measures of success. They have also often enjoyed success in love, friendship, self-respect, excitement and freedom. What is of critical importance is that a successful career is not a measure which, taken independently, correlates with high levels of satisfaction. Many of those displaying the highest levels of well-being were quite unwilling to put their family or friendships at risk in order to obtain professional success.

6. Mutual love

The most satisfied people appear to have loving relationships – whether married or not – which are equally balanced between the two people concerned. They spend more time with the one they love and often report that their relationships improved in their late thirties, forties or fifties.

No decision on any change in occupation should therefore be considered without the close involvement, support and agreement of one's partner.

7. Personal values

There are a number of values, such as being honest, loving and responsible, to which most people subscribe, yet the people most satisfied with their lives have additional values which vary according to their sex. Commonly, men most often value being fit, being open to new experiences, being courageous and being comfortable with intimacy and leadership.

On the other hand, highly satisfied women are often more ambitious, are knowledgeable, have a sense of humour, value fun and are open to new experiences.

One interesting factor is that in both cases the sexes have overcome some of the stereotyping from which most of us suffer. The women are more ambitious than the norm and the men are more comfortable with intimacy than are the majority of their sex.

8. Secure from criticism

Perhaps, not surprisingly, highly satisfied people tend not to be disturbed by criticism. They do not take criticism personally and are therefore less defensive, less likely to become angry, and less susceptible to psychosomatic disorders.

It appears that highly satisfied individuals are able to rationalise criticism, whether or not they accept it, in such a way that it never leaves them with sleepless nights.

9. Friendships

Individuals with a high level of well-being have significantly more friends. Therefore, they have more people to turn to for understanding or support. When considering a job change, this factor should not be under-estimated.

Friendships are important. And, as such, their loss must be weighed against any advantages offered by opportunities which require geographical relocation or work which might damage this type of relationship.

10. Anxiety levels

The anxieties of the majority – such as 'being too old to move', 'not progressing fast enough', and feeling insecure about ability – are not suffered to such a great degree by those who are highly satisfied. They do not, for example, become concerned about the speed at which their career is progressing until their late forties – which is much later than usual.

11. Age

Older people are frequently more contented than younger ones. The individuals most likely to be able to attain high levels of satisfaction are professional, married, mature people. The most troubled groups are probably those in their late teens or young married couples with young children.

12. Occupation

It is essential to find your ideal occupation if you are to achieve full job satisfaction. This is equally true whether individuals run small businesses or are self-employed, or are in the medical, legal, artistic or financial professions. Those in administrative occupations, trade union representatives or blue-collar workers often achieve high levels of satisfaction and feel they have realised their potential.

At the other end of the scale, people most likely to be dissatisfied are typically men in white-collar jobs, or those who have plateaued in middle management. Similarly, dissatisfied women are either housewives or in traditional secretarial jobs.

13. Marriage

Married people often appear to be more satisfied than those who are single. Research has shown that single women with small children, or ageing single men, are at the lowest end of the satisfaction scale. Of course, for many, being single is not a permanent state.

Summary

All of you have the potential to increase your satisfaction and move towards the optimum levels described here. A good place to begin is by trying to become more optimistic, more confident, and by starting to 'translate' difficulties into opportunities. We must begin by defining your own version of what the term 'success' means. We consider this more closely in the next chapter.

Case study: Graham

Graham began work in 1951 and believed that the company he had joined was to be his employer for life. He had left school with a good Schools Certificate and a Higher Schools Certificate. He gained wide international experience with the organisation, being involved mainly with marketing in the Far East and East Africa. He enjoyed his work and respected his employer who always treated him well.

The break, when it came in 1972, was not unexpected. It was, nevertheless, somewhat traumatic as he lost his sense of 'belonging'. Despite this he was not too upset as the way of life abroad had altered considerably. He and his wife were already thinking about returning to the UK, but he felt particularly vulnerable returning to a completely different working environment without any specialist qualifications.

Almost two years passed after their return to the UK before Graham took up a post in the Department of Health and Social Security, but that was only for a short period. He joined Customs and Excise in 1974 and has been there ever since. Of course, the transition from an overseas international commercial group to the Civil Service was considerable, but one similarity was that both organisations looked after their staff. More important, he found his new work interesting and challenging. He has become involved with the changing Customs role brought about by the European Community and with recent activities aimed at countering drug smuggling. He finds that there is scope for individuals to pursue their own particular areas of interest and use their initiative. He has been able to mould his job to his wishes.

Graham has enjoyed the change and feels it was successful. He wastes little time travelling to work and the job has surpassed all his expectations.

Chapter 5
Consider Yourself

This chapter seeks to provide additional insight for those considering taking a significant step towards changing their career. It may also be of interest to you if you are uncertain whether the career path you have chosen is the correct one. The chapter contains a number of exercises, the results of which are drawn together at the end. It is essential, therefore, that you examine and complete each exercise in the order in which it is printed. The results may otherwise be misleading.

Exercises such as these are not designed to provide you with ultimate answers to your career quandary. The authors treat 'pen and paper' exercises with scepticism when it is suggested that by simply ticking boxes or choosing alternatives you can accurately identify your perfect occupation. What these exercises do is provide a means and a framework within which you can consider your future in a relatively objective fashion. They will provide you with additional information about yourself and, in most cases, a new approach to determine which occupation will give you the highest possible level of satisfaction.

How do you normally make decisions?

The answer, of course, depends on what type of decision it is and whether you have had any experience of making such a decision, or a similar one, before. In most cases, it is common to have had past experience of identical or similar problems and your decision making is therefore based upon memory and reason rather than anything more complex.

Important decisions, or those made when you face a completely new situation, have to be determined by your conscious or subconscious values, attitudes and beliefs. Because you can manage, on a day-to-day basis, to make decisions which are almost always based on your knowledge of handling similar problems, you rarely need to refer back to these basic beliefs or values. Over a period of time, however, your values develop, change and often become indistinct. In order to maximise the effectiveness of your decision making and increase the chance of gaining as much as you can out of life – including time spent at work – you should take time to reappraise and update your awareness of the importance you place upon your values.

It is interesting to note that companies and organisations are usually sharply aware of these facts. They spend a significant amount of time and energy reassessing and bringing up to date their objectives, mission statements and purpose. Your values, and the priority you give them, provide you with your objectives. If you wish to maximise the satisfaction and enjoyment you obtain from life, developing a clearer awareness of your values will help you to make decisions consistently, confidently and effectively.

Value analysis can easily become a complex and difficult task. You may hold many more fundamental beliefs and values than you may at first appreciate. Achieving, or increasing, just one of them may reduce your satisfaction with many others. The first few exercises, therefore, are aimed at considering your values from different perspectives. The first two exercises are more effective if you can complete them with the assistance of the person in your life who knows you best. This will normally be your partner, but could equally be a close relative or friend. Do not concern yourself unduly if you have to do them on your own – you should still be able to gain much from completion of the exercises by yourself. If you are on your own, simply ignore the instructions for the other individual and complete the exercise by yourself.

Exercise 1: Personal values

This exercise is designed to help you to identify your most important values. Study the list of commonly held values on page 31. The exercise will help you to decide, initially, which values you believe are most important to you, which are of moderate importance, and which are of least importance.

In column 1 write 'A' against the values you believe are most important to you. You are limited to between four and six 'A' responses.

Then determine the values that are of least importance to you. Insert 'C' against these values, but you are limited to between three and eight 'C' responses.

The remaining values should, by elimination, be those that are of moderate importance to you. Please insert 'B' against these.

You should now have completed column 1. Fold the page over so that the

Exercise 1: Personal Values

Values	Column 3	Column 2	Column 1
HONESTY (sincerity, integrity)			
INDEPENDENCE (freedom, autonomy)			
CONTENTMENT (with oneself)			
CHALLENGE (new experiences, adventure)			
SECURITY (economic stability, adequate income)			
RELIGION (strong religious conviction)			
ACCOMPLISHMENT (professionalism, mastery)			
ORDER (conformity, stability)			
PRIDE (self-respect)			
CREATIVITY (innovation)			
AUTHORITY (influence over others, power)			
WINNING (risk-taking, competitiveness)			
DEVELOPMENT (achieving your potential)			
RESPECT (recognition, fame)			
AFFLUENCE (wealth)			
RELATIONSHIP (friendships)			
PROMOTION (status, seniority)			
BELONGING (involvement)			
AFFECTION (love, care)			
KNOWLEDGE (wisdom, understanding)			
FUN (relaxed lifestyle, pleasure)			
CO-OPERATION (team work)			
HEALTH (physical and mental)			
ACCOUNTABILITY (responsibility for results)			
LOYALTY (duty)			

FOLD HERE

whole of column 1, together with all your responses, is hidden. Then ask a friend, partner or relative to complete column 2 indicating what they perceive to be *your* values – the most important, those of moderate importance and the least important, following exactly the same rules for the maximum and minimum number of responses in each category.

Now comes the most important stage in the exercise. When column 2 has been completed for you, reveal column 1 to yourself and your 'assistant' and compare the results. Many values will obviously be identical and this important fact should enable you to feel comfortable that your own 'prioritisation' of values is a secure basis on which to progress. The interesting area, however, is where there is a difference between what you and your partner both grade as 'A' values. If either of you specified an 'A' value which does not agree with the other's assessment, discuss the reasons why each of you placed your ratings as you did.

To manage this quickly and easily, it is often helpful to quote examples of past behaviour which have led you thus to rank the value. Your previous behaviour will often have been based subconsciously on your values and so may illustrate them clearly and persuasively. When this discussion is complete, you should use column 3 to mark – with a pencil – your five top values with a letter 'A'. Then, mark with a 'B' the next three most important values.

We will come back to column 3 once you have both had a look at Exercise 2. If you are not tired after the first exercise, it is a good idea to move directly to Exercise 2.

Exercise 2: Alternatives

This is another exercise which you should attempt together. All you are asked to do is to consider each of the alternatives and tick whichever one you feel you identify with more closely. For example, do you think of yourself as more of a friend than an adviser? Tick the box next to the definition which you feel suits you more than the alternative. This should take you no more than two minutes. When this is done pass the book to your partner who, by following the instructions on page 44, can help you to complete the second stage. *It will devalue the purpose of the exercise if you read these instructions before completing stage one.*

Exercise 2: Alternatives
Do you think of yourself as more: (please tick box)

☐ Friend or Adviser? ☐

☐ Team Game or Track Event? ☐

☐ Participator or Demonstrator? ☐

☐ Borrower or Lender? ☐

☐ An Adventure Holiday or a Cruise?
☐

☐ Provincial or Cosmopolitan?
☐

☐ A Cliff or a Desert? ☐

☐ An Express Train or a Ski Lift? ☐

☐ French or Norwegian? ☐

☐ A Penthouse or a Beach Bungalow?
☐

☐ Money or Valuables? ☐

☐ At the Top or at the Side? ☐

☐ An Explorer or a Mountain Rescuer?
☐

Exercise 3: Value prioritisation

Before beginning Exercise 3, review the top values you identified in Exercise 1. You may wish to amend them following the outcome of Exercise 2. Before finally confirming your top priorities, take a moment to decide whether they are all 'primary' values or whether some are 'secondary'; that is, some of the values may support others. For example, you may have both health and independence shown as high priority values. However, you may value health only because it is essential to provide you with the independence that is of primary importance. Similarly, affluence may be valued in order to provide security. If you find that you have any of these secondary values in your top list, replace them with other primary values.

You are now asked to prioritise these final values. Although all these values are extremely important to you, if you can now place them in order of importance you will be able to complete the subsequent exercises.

Step 1. Imagine that you can guarantee that you will make the right career decision, but the cost is one of your values – discard it.

Step 2. A friend is in hospital and you can cure him or her instantaneously but the cost is one of the remaining values – discard it.

Step 3. Cancer can become totally curable, but the cost is one of the remaining values – discard it.

Step 4. You now have only two remaining values. The greenhouse effect can be reversed instantaneously by the surrender of one of those values – discard it.

When you have overcome the after-effects of the stress involved in that last exercise, you can complete the value prioritisation sheet opposite. Place your most important value as 1, the next most important as 2, etc.

You can now consider to what extent each of your values is being satisfied. If you are completely fulfilled in regard to a particular value, award that value a 100 per cent score. If you believe that you could double the amount of satisfaction you are obtaining at present, give that value 50 per cent, etc, so providing a range from total dissatisfaction at 0 per cent to complete satisfaction at 100 per cent.

The next step is to split the percentage score for each of your values, according to where you obtain that satisfaction. If you have given one of

Exercise 3: Value prioritisation

	Values	Current Satisfaction %	Work	Home
1.		=	+	
2.		=	+	
3.		=	+	
4.		=	+	
5.		=	+	
Total		=	+	

First: What is your current level of satisfaction, as a percentage?
Second: Split between work and home.

your values an 80 per cent score, but you obtain most of your satisfaction of that value at work, you might estimate that 60 per cent of the 80 per cent satisfaction is obtained at work and 20 per cent at home. In this manner, complete the two remaining columns on your value prioritisation sheet.

Finally, you can total the scores for work and home. Do these results contain any surprises?

This exercise has drawn our investigation of values to a close for the time being. We will return to this in the next chapter.

Exercise 4: Job dimensions

This exercise studies the dimensions which are contained within most jobs. The dimensions are listed down each side of page 38. The left-hand and right-hand lists are two extremes of the same dimension. Your task is to examine each line, as shown below. Please complete Step 1 before moving on.

Step 1. Known occupation.
Working steadily down page 38 consider each dimension for an occupation you know well. Obviously, choose your current job, unless you are out of work or just about to return to work, when you should pick a previous occupation of which you had reasonable experience. Mark with an 'O' the column which most accurately describes where on that dimension your known occupation falls. For example, taking the dimension ranging between 'supervising many' and 'no supervision', if you supervised a large group of people insert your 'O' in the column headed HD – Highly Descriptive on the left-hand side. Alternatively, if you only supervised one person, or your supervision was not direct or formal, you should insert your 'O' in the column D – Descriptive, which is second from the right, as shown in this example:

		HD	D	=	D	HD	
1.	Supervise many						No supervision
2.	Teamwork						Work independently
3.	Customer contact						No customer contact
4.	Work in large organisation						Work alone
5.	Produce goods						Provide a service

Try to avoid the equal sign 'in the middle' as much as possible but not to the extent of exaggeration.

When you have completed this step for all the dimensions, join up all your marks, leaving a profile for that particular occupation, as shown below:

		HD	D	=	D	HD	
1.	Supervise many				Q		No supervision
2.	Teamwork					O	Work independently
3.	Customer contact	O					No customer contact
4.	Work in large organisation				O		Work alone
5.	Produce goods	O					Provide a service

Step 2. Ideal job.
This is the most important part of the exercise. Please mark with an 'X' the column for each dimension which would ideally describe your *perfect* occupation.

As shown in another example below, if in Step 1 you marked the descriptive column for 'Supervise many', but you would prefer to work most on your own, insert an 'X' in one of the right-hand columns. Work down the page in the same manner. When this is complete, use a different coloured pen or pencil and join up your ideal profile.

		HD	D	=	D	HD	
1.	Supervise many		O		X		No supervision
2.	Teamwork	X				O	Work independently
3.	Customer contact	X				O	No customer contact
4.	Work in large organisation		X		O		Work alone
5.	Produce goods				X O		Provide a service

Exercise 4: Job dimensions

Key: HD – Highly Descriptive, D – Descriptive, = In the middle

		HD	D	=	D	HD	
1.	Supervise many						No supervision
2.	Teamwork						Work independently
3.	Customer contact						No customer contact
4.	Work in large organisation						Work alone
5.	Produce goods						Provide a service
6.	Fixed salary						Paid by results
7.	Flexitime						Fixed hours
8.	Routine work						Lots of surprises
9.	Lots of travel						No travel
10.	Closely managed						Managed from afar
11.	Work with same group						Work with different people
12.	Work indoors						Work outside
13.	Highly technical						Not technical
14.	Little innovation						Considerable innovation
15.	Short work cycles						Long work projects
16.	Low financial risk						High financial risk
17.	High attention to detail						Low attention to detail
18.	High specialisation						Low specialisation
19.	High visibility						Low visibility
20.	Extended working hours						9–5 job
21.	Many deadlines						Few deadlines
22.	Others depend on you						Little dependence
23.	Highly structured						Little structure
		HD	D	=	D	HD	

Exercise 5: Personal qualities

This exercise employs the same principle as Exercise 4, but applies it to your personal qualities. You can complete it yourself, but the help of your 'assistant' or someone else who has known you at work may be useful. You can either work together, discussing each dimension in turn, or work on the exercise separately and compare your results afterwards. The latter method probably has a more objective outcome.

Consider each dimension in turn. Work steadily down the page, ticking the column which most accurately describes your personal quality level.

Again, avoid the 'equal' column as far as possible. When you have completed all 23 dimensions, join each of your results as shown in the example below:

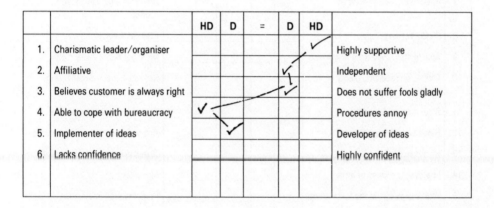

		HD	D	=	D	HD	
1.	Charismatic leader/organiser					✓	Highly supportive
2.	Affiliative				✓		Independent
3.	Believes customer is always right				✓		Does not suffer fools gladly
4.	Able to cope with bureaucracy	✓					Procedures annoy
5.	Implementer of ideas		✓				Developer of ideas
6.	Lacks confidence						Highly confident

Note that the dimensions are not opposites in every case, yet you are being asked to identify which describes you most closely. Do your best, as the next exercise allows you to interpret the results intelligently.

Exercise 5: Personal qualities

Key: HD – Highly Descriptive, D – Descriptive, = In the middle

		HD	D	=	D	HD	
1.	Enjoys organising others						Never tells others what to do
2.	Affiliative						Independent
3.	Believes customer is always right						Does not suffer fools gladly
4.	Able to cope with bureaucracy						Procedures annoy
5.	Implementer of ideas						Developer of ideas
6.	Lacks confidence						Highly confident
7.	Fixed work routine difficult						Able to manage fixed work routine
8.	Dislikes change						Change oriented
9.	Able to stay away from home						Must get home every night
10.	Thrives on receiving plenty of direction						Resents constant monitoring
11.	Slow to make friends						Enjoys meeting new people
12.	Hates bad weather/winter						Any weather has its enjoyments
13.	Methodical and accurate						Speed is better than accuracy
14.	Improves the ideas of others						Innovator
15.	Works urgently (at the last minute)						Prepares well in advance
16.	Hates to lose						Enjoys gambling
17.	Reads every word						Only reads the headlines
18.	Has expertise						Has generalist background
19.	Enjoys giving presentations						Does not like to be judged
20.	Work is more important than home life						Home life is more important than work
21.	Conscientious						Prefers flexible schedules
22.	Enjoys challenges						Hates being rushed
23.	Dependable						Free spirit
		HD	D	=	D	HD	

Exercise 6: Strengths and weaknesses

Here again you have the job dimensions chart. The difference is that you are now able to compare your abilities with the occupation you consider to be ideal.

The purpose of this exercise is to assist you in identifying an occupation which is not just 'ideal', but is also practicable. Everybody has strengths and weaknesses, yet we are all able to cope with one job or another. However, you must compare your abilities with those required by your ideal job.

The exercise requires you to transfer all your 'Xs' from Exercise 4 and join them together with straight lines. Next transfer all the ticks from Exercise 5 on to the same page, as shown in the following example:

		HD	D	=	D	HD	
1.	Supervise many				X	✓	No supervision
2.	Teamwork	X			✓		Work independently
3.	Customer contact	X			✓		No customer contact
4.	Work in large organisation	✓	X				Work alone
5.	Produce goods		✓		X		Provide a service

You must now study every dimension where your 'Xs' and ticks appear in different columns. A difference of one column is insignificant and you can usually ignore it. Where there is any greater difference you should ask yourself the following questions.

How did you interpret Exercise 5? The job dimensions in Exercise 4 were intended to relate directly to the personal quality dimensions in Exercise 5. However, did you interpret them differently? If the gap is caused by a different interpretation, simply ignore it and move on. If this is honestly not the case, you must ask yourself whether your ideal job is a practical aspiration.

If you need to reconsider your ideal occupation, you must now adjust your 'Xs' to accommodate these changes.

Exercise 6: Strengths and weaknesses

Key: HD – Highly Descriptive, D – Descriptive, = In the middle

		HD	D	=	D	HD	
1.	Supervise many						No supervision
2.	Teamwork						Work independently
3.	Customer contact						No customer contact
4.	Work in large organisation						Work alone
5.	Produce goods						Provide a service
6.	Fixed salary						Paid by results
7.	Flexitime						Fixed hours
8.	Routine work						Lots of surprises
9.	Lots of travel						No travel
10.	Closely managed						Managed from afar
11.	Work with same group						Work with different people
12.	Work indoors						Work outside
13.	Highly technical						Not technical
14.	Little innovation						Considerable innovation
15.	Short work cycles						Long work projects
16.	Low financial risk						High financial risk
17.	High attention to detail						Low attention to detail
18.	High specialisation						Low specialisation
19.	High visibility						Low visibility
20.	Extended working hours						9–5 job
21.	Many deadlines						Few deadlines
22.	Others depend on you						Little dependence
23.	Highly structured						Little structure
		HD	D	=	D	HD	

Job decision making

Please transfer your top values from Exercise 3 into the values column. Weight each of your values in comparison with 100 per cent given to the top one. For example, if value 2 is very nearly as important to you, give it 95 per cent, if it is far lower give it 70 per cent. Do this for each value.

Then consider your top value for each job, completing column A in the job that satisfies that value the most with a 100 per cent mark. Complete column A for the other two jobs with a proportionate mark. Repeat this for each value, giving 100 per cent to the job which satisfies it the most.

Next complete column B for each value and job by multiplying the value percentage by the figure in column B for that job. This provides you with a weighted result. Finally, add up each column B. The results should be written in the total boxes. The highest total 'wins'. Any surprises?

Values	Value %	Known job		Alternative job 1		Alternative job 2	
		A	B	A	B	A	B
1.							
2.							
3.							
4.							
5.							
Total							

You are now in a strong position to consider a whole range of occupations. Some are shown in the next chapter, but there are many others, too numerous to be included. To examine the alternatives proceed as follows:

1. Take any possible job or occupational area and place it within the dimensions shown in Exercise 6. See how closely it matches your ideal and realistic profile.

2. Having completed this step you must return to the earlier personal values exercises. On page 43 we have set out a method by which you can identify how much job satisfaction you might obtain from any possible future occupation. Begin by studying a known job. This identifies whether or not you can improve your job satisfaction.

3. If any chosen occupational area passes all these tests it is seriously worth considering and taking further. Remember, however, that while these exercises have provided a means by which you can examine your options objectively, there is no guarantee of success. Do not, therefore, place all your hopes and aspirations in one particular area. Ideally, you should take two or three areas, all of which pass these tests. You have had to make a number of assumptions so far. Only by further investigating each area will you be able to gain sufficient knowledge to make the right final decision.

Instructions for Exercise 2

To be read only by the assistant
The purpose of this exercise is to provide an alternative view of the participant's values.

When he or she has completed the list of alternatives on page 33, take the list and, beginning at the top, ask the participant the following question for each alternative:

'Why did you see yourself more as a . . . than as a . . .?'

The answers you are seeking must contain value statements. For example, 'I feel more French because I value romance and affection.'

Do *not* evaluate the answers at this stage; continue to ask for explanations until you have at least one value for each alternative.

Write down the values on the right-hand side of the page. When this is complete, pass the book back to your partner and discuss the outcome.

There may be values contained in this list that were not generated by Exercise 1, or a particular value may have appeared a few times. If either of these situations arises, consider whether the top five values need amending.

Chapter 6

Your Choice of Occupation

We hope that you can now look at realistic opportunities and make a career decision objectively. Remember that each year 1 person in 12 changes his or her occupation. One important decision to be made is whether to apply for a post with another employer or consider self-employment. This chapter is aimed at assisting those seeking fresh employment. You can now undertake a 'matching' analysis in order to compare your job requirements, as identified in Exercises 5 and 6, with a number of possible careers. (Self-employment is covered in Chapter 9.)

The range of occupations

A selection of occupations follows, from hairdresser to landscape architect. The careers are grouped into four sections:

    A. Nationwide Organisations
    B. Construction, Housing and Transport
    C. Hotel, Leisure and Retail Industries
    D. Professional Services

A list of the occupations is given below.

This chapter provides you with the opportunity to gain detailed information about each occupation, career or profession. For most occupations, a questionnaire has been compiled by the relevant organisation, eg The Institute of Chartered Accountants in England and Wales.

Grouping of questionnaires and contributions from employers and professional associations

    A. Nationwide Organisations
        British Council 48
        British Gas 51
        Civil Service (including Customs and Excise Officers and Probation Service) 52

Where a questionnaire is not appropriate for major employers, such as the

National Health Service or the Civil Service, we have prepared a description of the range of occupations and have agreed this with the organisation. This has been supplemented by career details of specific occupations such as physiotherapists with the NHS or probation officers within the Civil Service. Other employers such as British Gas have prepared their own contributions. Additional background material has been provided where necessary.

To help you further in making your choice, we have prepared an appropriate job dimension sheet for each occupational area, which can be matched up with Chapter 5.

When you have identified a number of possible areas of interest, we suggest that you write to the contact point of the organisations concerned to obtain further details. This should be done before you eliminate any possibilities. When you have received the information requested, reappraise the position and then take your favoured possibilities a step further by arranging to meet the person in each organisation who has supplied the career details. In some cases you may be able to visit a local employer in your chosen field of interest. For instance, if you have obtained the descriptive literature regarding radiography, ring the Radiography Department of your local hospital and ask for an appointment for an informal chat.

Don't be afraid to ask for help. Most people love talking about their jobs! By following this process through, you will gradually eliminate certain options until you are left with a manageable shortlist. The sample of occupations we have included cannot, for obvious reasons, be exhaustive. If your career search throws up a possibility closely allied to one of our examples, consult the careers literature in the reference section of your local library.

You are now in a position to decide whether you need training or whether you can begin the job search, in which case consult Chapter 7 or Chapter 8.

A. Nationwide Organisations

The British Council
If you were to stop over in Jakarta en route to Bali, you would find a large British Council office serving Indonesia. As well as a comprehensive library of reference and fiction books, you would see an information centre and a busy teaching centre with Council staff. They are bringing Indonesian

Job dimensions: British Council Officer

Key: HD – Highly Descriptive, D – Descriptive, = In the middle

		HD	D	=	D	HD	
1.	Supervise many		X	X			No supervision
2.	Teamwork		X				Work independently
3.	Customer contact	X					No customer contact
4.	Work in large organisation			X			Work alone
5.	Produce goods					X	Provide a service
6.	Fixed salary	X					Paid by results
7.	Flexitime	X					Fixed hours
8.	Routine work		X	X			Lots of surprises
9.	Lots of travel		X	X			No travel
10.	Closely managed		X	X			Managed from afar
11.	Work with same group		X	X			Work with different people
12.	Work indoors	X					Work outside
13.	Highly technical			X			Not technical
14.	Little innovation			X			Considerable innovation
15.	Short work cycles		X	X			Long work projects
16.	Low financial risk	X					High financial risk
17.	High attention to detail	X					Low attention to detail
18.	High specialisation			X			Low specialisation
19.	High visibility	X					Low visibility
20.	Extended working hours			X			9–5 job
21.	Many deadlines		X				Few deadlines
22.	Others depend on you	X					Little dependence
23.	Highly structured			X			Little structure
		HD	D	=	D	HD	

students' knowledge of English up to a standard which would allow them to benefit from study at educational institutions in the UK. If you are brave enough to get off the concrete jungle tourist route between Singapore and Hong Kong to visit Borneo, you will find small, but effective, Council offices in Sabah and Sarawak. You will probably see, as you enter, posters from British universities extolling their virtues, details of British Council bursaries for Malaysians to study in the UK and an announcement of a visiting British musical group on a cultural tour. Today, all the Council's 127 libraries around the world make about 8 million loans a year to a membership of 513,000 people. Modern information technology is increasingly in evidence and many of the libraries are purpose-designed centres with film and video stocks, software demonstration equipment and on-line access to British and international databases, such as BLAISE, BEST and Dialog.

The majority of people in the 30+ age group apply for clerical and administrative posts in the Home Career Service which are open to applicants with GCE O-level or equivalent passes in English and mathematics and a good general education. Candidates with GCE A levels or equivalent are welcome to apply, and there are some vacancies suitable for recent graduates with little experience of administrative work. There is much personal contact in setting up training programmes for students and visitors from overseas and dealing with their welfare. All such posts are based in Manchester. There is a range of clerical, typing and registry posts. Apart from the main offices in London and Manchester, there are 19 smaller offices in university towns throughout the UK. In these, there is more regular contact with the public. For those with graduate and similar professional qualifications, plus two years' relevant work experience, there may be occasional vacancies at higher grades. People with experience in teaching, libraries, information science, computing, publishing, etc, will have an advantage. Former VSOs and others with work experience overseas should include such details on their application forms. Candidates up to 55 years of age will be considered.

For the Overseas Career Service entry qualifications are more stringent – either a postgraduate or a professional qualification plus work experience is required. The upper age limit for the Overseas Career Service applicants is 50, though the upper age range of recruits tends to be around 40. Entry into the Home Career Service provides the opportunity for advancement and possibly the chance to travel overseas.

Case studies

A female clerical assistant was based in London for three years on personnel work dealing with teachers on contract overseas. She was then posted to Zagreb. On her marriage, she returned to London as a home serving member of staff. After a varied and satisfying career linked with promotion through five grades, she became Head of the Personnel Department, and subsequently Director of the Libraries, Books and Information Division.

A graduate joined at the general administration grade. His first job was making travel arrangements for British specialists in medicine and education being sent overseas by the Council. Later he had responsibility for young British scientists posted to India. Soon he was dealing with Chinese postgraduate scientists brought over to study in the UK. Further career changes gave him the opportunity to make duty visits to Austria (UN), Burma and Thailand. During this period, the Council paid a proportion of his fees so he could take an MA in Commonwealth history.

The Council also offers opportunities for people to serve in contract posts overseas. Contracts are generally for between two and three years and will require particular qualifications. Most opportunities are for teachers and advisers, the majority in English language teaching. These are advertised in the national press.

For further information contact the British Council at 10 Spring Gardens, London SW1A 2BN; 071-930 8466. (Ask for Recruitment Unit, Personnel Department.)

British Gas

The main business of British Gas is to buy, transmit and distribute natural gas through a transmission system 230,000 km (145,000 miles) long to 17.7 million domestic, commercial and industrial customers in Great Britain.

In addition to supplying gas, the company provides a wide range of complementary services, including the sale, installation and servicing of appliances, and it is committed to ensuring that gas appliances are installed and used safely.

As part of its strategy for growth, British Gas is creating a major international exploration and production business with interests in both gas and oil and is currently operating in 17 countries. The company's expertise in all aspects of the gas business is internationally recognised and provides a multitude of opportunities for selling British Gas products and services to both developed and developing nations. This success continues to depend on the 80,000 men and women employed throughout the world. Their commitment and hard work in areas as diverse as finance, marketing, personnel, customer service, customer accounting, research and technology, production and supply, are vital in continually improving the standard of service to customers and to the future growth of the company.

In ensuring that it has the skilled workforce to meet these challenges, British Gas is committed to providing equal employment opportunities for all employees irrespective of gender, race or disability. The company continually reviews its recruitment and retention policies to ensure that they provide facilities for equal development. The company has a skills retention programme, a career break scheme and maternity leave arrangements which exceed statutory requirements.

A firm commitment to the ongoing training of staff is demonstrated by the company's Further Education Policy and Management Training Framework, while the introduction of Competence Based Training, which establishes clear definitions of learning goals, enables individuals to govern their own development.

British Gas is an integral part of the community it serves. It supports a variety of community activities both in the UK and overseas. These range from sponsorship of the arts, large-scale community projects and sporting events through to localised support for individual groups and people.

For more information about career opportunities with British Gas contact the Personnel Department in your region.

The Civil Service
With more than half a million employees, the Civil Service is both one of the biggest employers in the UK and one of the most geographically spread. Civil servants work in all government departments, managing people, businesses and resources on a vast scale. They are expected to be politically neutral and objective in their duties. Their role remains the same whatever the policies or priorities of the government of the day.

It must be emphasised that the Civil Service is keen to recruit both 'generalists' and professionals/specialists in their mid- or late careers. People who have gained qualifications and experience and women 'returners' will find their applications welcomed.

The main source of entry for 'generalists' is as an Executive Officer.

'Generalists'
Executive Officers (EOs) form the backbone of junior and middle

management. They carry out a wide variety of tasks requiring responsibility and initiative. Most EO work falls into one or more of the following broad areas:

(a) Management of junior staff is a major element in many departments. The tasks include allocating, monitoring and controlling work; training, appraising and motivating junior staff.

(b) Casework involves the application of rules and regulations to particular situations. EOs must exercise their judgement fairly and objectively.

(c) Contact with the public by correspondence, telephone or in person is a major part of many jobs in Customs and Excise, the Department of Employment and the Department of Social Security. EOs need to present an acceptable image and deal effectively with people and organisations.

(d) Administration covers diverse activities including: personnel; general enquiries and correspondence; support and research for senior officers.

(e) Information technology (IT) embraces computer operations, programming and systems analysis. Most of this work is done by EOs and higher grades in the Administration Group. The Civil Service is Britain's largest user of computers, with advanced systems and development techniques. Training may be given, including help towards qualifications for membership of the British Computer Society.

(f) Accountancy represents an important and growing area of work. EOs who have the aptitude and commitment are able to apply for training under sponsored schemes for a professional accountancy qualification.

Some departments have posts which equate to EO but which involve more specialised work. These include the Inland Revenue (Revenue Executive and Valuation Technician), Home Office (Immigration Officer) and Department of Trade (Examiner in Insolvency).

Executive Officer appointments
Candidates up to 50 years of age will be considered. Graduates with degrees in all disciplines are eligible to apply. The minimum qualifications are two A levels and three GCSEs (or equivalent).

Job dimensions: Civil Service Executive Officer

Key: HD – Highly Descriptive, D – Descriptive, = In the middle

		HD	D	=	D	HD	
1.	Supervise many			X			No supervision
2.	Teamwork		X				Work independently
3.	Customer contact	X	X				No customer contact
4.	Work in large organisation	X		X			Work alone
5.	Produce goods					X	Provide a service
6.	Fixed salary	X					Paid by results
7.	Flexitime			X			Fixed hours
8.	Routine work	X					Lots of surprises
9.	Lots of travel			X			No travel
10.	Closely managed		X				Managed from afar
11.	Work with same group	X					Work with different people
12.	Work indoors	X					Work outside
13.	Highly technical			X			Not technical
14.	Little innovation	X					Considerable innovation
15.	Short work cycles				X		Long work projects
16.	Low financial risk	X					High financial risk
17.	High attention to detail	X					Low attention to detail
18.	High specialisation			X			Low specialisation
19.	High visibility		X	X			Low visibility
20.	Extended working hours					X	9–5 job
21.	Many deadlines				X		Few deadlines
22.	Others depend on you			X			Little dependence
23.	Highly structured	X					Little structure
		HD	D	=	D	HD	

Applications should only be sent in response to an advertisement in the national or local press.

High flyers can consider entry to the Civil Service as an Administration Trainee but there are only approximately 100 vacancies each year and the competition is tough for this fast stream.

Professional staff and specialists

Accountants will find that the government accounting service comprises 750 qualified accountants and approximately 500 trainee accountants. There are no age limits for accountancy posts and in recent years female applicants have comprised over 28 per cent of appointments. Staff work in over 40 departments and are encouraged to participate in a wide range of training courses.

Engineers. There are openings for engineers of every description, both qualified and trainee. Women with engineering degrees, in particular, are encouraged to achieve chartered status.

Surveyors. Five hundred vacancies occur each year in various departments, such as the Property Services Agency, the Defence Estate Service and the Valuation Office. There is an outstanding training programme.

Economists work in 20 different departments. Macro- and micro-economics are covered. Most vacancies are in London but there are some in Sheffield and Edinburgh. Individuals have the chance to apply their skills to a wide range of intellectually stimulating and socially worthwhile issues.

There are other vacancies for librarians, lawyers, statisticians, inspectors of taxes, press and publicity officers, scientists, etc. If you are interested in a career in the European Community, ask for the booklet 'The European Fast-stream'.

Members of the public whose mental picture of the Civil Service has been distorted by the *Yes, Minister* TV series may well be surprised to read a booklet called 'Made to Measure'. This is published by HM Treasury and spells out the dramatic changes that the public service has had to make to compete for staff and the flexibility of the working arrangements. For example, some part-timers at the VAT Centre in Southend work a two-week alternating pattern. At the port of Dover part-time evening work is being introduced as the port needs staffing around the clock.

Occupational pension benefits have always been a key factor in attracting personnel to the public service but these benefits are now available to part-time workers.

Former civil servants with a good record will find that reinstatement is a fast route back. Home working is a pattern of work which a number of departments are developing successfully. The Ministry of Defence, for example, has introduced a scheme for staff whose family commitments might otherwise make it difficult for them to continue to work. Job-share schemes are also in operation.

The excellent pension scheme is non-contributory. Some departments have childcare provision and holiday play schemes.

Because of the diversity of work in the Civil Service, only a few examples are given, but we include the Probation Service on page 58 and Customs and Excise below. There is a relevant case study on page 28.

For further information, write to the Recruitment and Assessment Services Agency, Alençon Link, Basingstoke, Hants RG21 1JB, stating the type of post which interests you.

For posts involving general clerical duties at Administrative Assistant/Administrative Officer level, contact your Jobcentre, and watch for advertisements in the local newspaper.

A married woman's report on home work
Mrs J H, who works for the Ministry of Defence, said:

> 'I wanted to return to work after my child was born, and working part-time has suited me. But being able to work at home for some of the time has made it much easier for me to combine my career and my role as a parent. My job in personnel policy is mainly project work and I can do much of this just as well at home with the help of a small computer and a printer provided by the department. I think the Civil Service is giving serious consideration to what it can do to retain its experienced staff and help them through the years when childcare responsibilities are particularly heavy – schemes like this make all the difference.'

Customs and Excise

Customs and Excise Officer
The Customs and Excise department has around 27,000 staff. The majority work on VAT collection and are office based. About 600 are involved in specialist investigation work and fewer than 10,000 work at customs posts or outdoor duties visiting firms.

There are headquarters in London, Southend (the largest), Manchester

Job dimensions: Customs and Excise Officer

Key: HD – Highly Descriptive, D – Descriptive, = In the middle

		HD	D	=	D	HD	
1.	Supervise many			X			No supervision
2.	Teamwork	X					Work independently
3.	Customer contact	X					No customer contact
4.	Work in large organisation	X		X			Work alone
5.	Produce goods					X	Provide a service
6.	Fixed salary			X			Paid by results
7.	Flexitime	X					Fixed hours
8.	Routine work	X				X	Lots of surprises
9.	Lots of travel			X			No travel
10.	Closely managed			X			Managed from afar
11.	Work with same group				X		Work with different people
12.	Work indoors	X				X	Work outside
13.	Highly technical		X				Not technical
14.	Little innovation			X			Considerable innovation
15.	Short work cycles				X		Long work projects
16.	Low financial risk		X				High financial risk
17.	High attention to detail	X					Low attention to detail
18.	High specialisation		X				Low specialisation
19.	High visibility	X					Low visibility
20.	Extended working hours			X			9–5 job
21.	Many deadlines			X			Few deadlines
22.	Others depend on you		X				Little dependence
23.	Highly structured		X				Little structure
		HD	D	=	D	HD	

and Liverpool. Approximately 900 offices are based around the country, at airports and seaports and in VAT and excise collecting centres. The number of staff in each varies from 5 to 1000. The department has a wide variety of opportunities. Most vacancies occur in VAT work. There are good promotion opportunities and it may be possible to move to vacancies in different parts of the country. Management development programmes are available for those with proven potential.

Personal characteristics
It is important to be totally honest. Customs and excise officers must be able to build a relationship with businesses based on respect and trust and explain regulations and decisions to them with tact. A clear speaking voice and a high standard of written English are useful. They must be able to interpret accounts and make calculations, applying regulations correctly. Logical problem-solving and the ability to make decisions are essential. They must pay close attention to detail and notice inconsistencies.

A firm manner is required and the confidence to enforce legal require-ments. Customs officers must be able to work as part of a team. Those collecting VAT and duty need the self-confidence to visit clients on their own. Persistence is important. It takes skill and experience to spot deception.

Officers work in offices, at business premises and in customs halls. They may visit companies at their premises. Some work may be dirty and hazardous.

On page 53 we described the entry procedure for Executive Officers, which is a possible method of joining the Customs and Excise department but this cannot be guaranteed. Further information may be obtained from Customs and Excise, Personnel Division A(3), HM Customs and Excise, 6th Floor Central, New Kings Beam House, 22 Upper Ground, London SE1 9PJ; 071-865 5776.

The Probation Service
The government plans to make substantial changes to the criminal justice system. The proposals are intended to ensure that only the most serious offenders are sent to prison. More offenders will be given community service. The ideas behind the government's White Paper will affect the way in which the Probation Service works.

Probation orders will become a sentence of the courts, and offenders will carry out community service under the supervision of a probation officer.

The government's new approach to the sentencing of offenders will require changes to the probation organisation, which will certainly have to expand in the next few years to meet the new demands on the service. (No decisions have yet been made on any reorganisation.)

The main aim of the Probation Service is to help offenders to stop offending. The community penalties provided by the Probation Service will make tough demands on offenders. But a community work sentence does not mean 'suffering in the community'. The emphasis is on constructive work to help offenders:

- recognise the effects of their offending;
- tackle the problems which underlie their offending;
- change their behaviour, and
- make reparation to the community.

Probation officers will continue to need social work skills. They have to be able to combine care and control in order to exercise caring authority over those under their supervision. But the 'skills base' of probation work will have to broaden. Increasingly, the new approach to probation work will demand skills in management and organisation: probation officers must be able to manage resources, to organise their own time and workloads, to draw effectively on the resources and skills of others around them, and to motivate any staff under their direct control. Probation officers should not see themselves as exclusive providers of services and facilities. The voluntary and private sectors have skills and experience on which the service can draw.

Every year, men and women join the Probation Service from a variety of different backgrounds, ethnic origins and walks of life. Some have gained their professional qualifications after completing full-time education or after a period as ancillary or voluntary workers with area probation services. Some have transferred from related professional work such as the social services. Others have qualified after spending much of their working lives in fields far removed from social work or the public service.

What they have in common is a concern for the individual and a commitment to the wider community, a commitment which comes face to face with some of the most difficult problems involving crime and conciliation in society.

If you think you can tackle this work, write to the Home Office for a copy of their booklet 'Face to Face' (Probation Service Division, The Home Office, Queen Anne's Gate, London SW1H 9AT). This booklet covers the wide

Questionnaire: Probation Service

1. Name and address of organisation

   Probation Service Division, Home Office, Queen Anne's Gate, London SW1H 9AT

2. Telephone no

   071-273 3520

3. Fax no

   071-273 4078

4. Typically, for what job(s) does membership of your organisation qualify a person?

   We are not an organisation with members but we sponsor students with a view to their joining the Probation Service – we can also provide information about careers in that service

5. Up to what age is it practical for our readers to consider a career change to these occupations?

   There is no specific upper age limit but realistically up to the mid-forties is probably the limit for beginning a qualifying course

6. Minimum education standards necessary

   To become a probation officer you must hold a Certificate of Qualification in Social Work (CQSW) or a Diploma in Social Work (DipSW). (See para 10 below.)

7. Qualifying examinations

   —

8. Essential experience

   —

9. Desirable experience

   Previous work with the Probation Service as an auxiliary or as a volunteer

10. Training available (course(s) and examples of existing providers)

    (a) Full-time

    (b) Part-time

    (c) Correspondence course

    (d) Distance learning

    (e) Other

11. Additional comments (government grants and other initiatives for mature students, bursaries, etc)

    A number of universities and polytechnics provide courses with a probation option leading to the grant of a CQSW or DipSW. The Home Office sponsors over 300 students each year on these courses

Job dimensions: Probation Officer

Key: HD – Highly Descriptive, D – Descriptive, = In the middle

		HD	D	=	D	HD	
1.	Supervise many		X				No supervision
2.	Teamwork	X					Work independently
3.	Customer contact	X					No customer contact
4.	Work in large organisation			X			Work alone
5.	Produce goods					X	Provide a service
6.	Fixed salary	X					Paid by results
7.	Flexitime		X				Fixed hours
8.	Routine work		X——		—X		Lots of surprises
9.	Lots of travel		X——		—X		No travel
10.	Closely managed		X				Managed from afar
11.	Work with same group		X				Work with different people
12.	Work indoors		X——		—X		Work outside
13.	Highly technical		X				Not technical
14.	Little innovation		X				Considerable innovation
15.	Short work cycles				X		Long work projects
16.	Low financial risk		X——		—X		High financial risk
17.	High attention to detail	X					Low attention to detail
18.	High specialisation	X					Low specialisation
19.	High visibility	X					Low visibility
20.	Extended working hours					X	9–5 job
21.	Many deadlines	X					Few deadlines
22.	Others depend on you	X					Little dependence
23.	Highly structured		X				Little structure
		HD	D	=	D	HD	

range of duties of the Probation Service, contains fascinating case histories regarding the treatment of offenders, describes working methods and analyses the qualities required. Foremost comes maturity of outlook and emotional maturity. The Home Office already sponsors over 300 students each year on professional courses for the necessary qualifications.

Libraries and Information Services

We live in the age of information. For example, the public needs information about job vacancies, regulations, leisure activities, current affairs, and so on. Doctors and nurses need medical and scientific information. Lawyers need all kinds of information ranging from current affairs to specific law reports or statutes. Business people and companies need information about sources of finance and legislation to survive in a competitive, fast-moving world. Information is not simply data or facts, but also ideas, opinions, concepts and cultural values. Nowadays, this broad range of information is presented not only in books but also through the audio-visual media (audio and video disc or tape) and computer networks.

Apart from local public library and information services, libraries or information centres are maintained by colleges, polytechnics and universities, schools, industrial and commercial organisations, hospitals, professional practices (lawyers, engineers, accountants), research institutes, government departments, radio and TV companies, etc. In fact, library and information services managed by professionals exist in every sector of human activity.

A great variety of satisfying job opportunities exists not only for qualified chartered librarians and information managers but also for enthusiastic support staff in clerical and administrative capacities.

Questionnaire: Librarianship and Information Science

1. Name and address of organisation	Education Department, The Library Association, 7 Ridgmount Street, London WC1E 7AE
2. Telephone no	071-636 7543
3. Fax no	071-436 7218
4. Typically, for what job(s) does membership of your organisation qualify a person?	Anyone can be a member. Chartered Membership, however, is open to graduates who satisfy the Association's criteria for admission to its professional register. Chartered Membership qualifies graduates for professional posts and advancement to managerial positions in this field

5. Up to what age is it practical for our readers to consider a career change to these occupations?

Depending on level of qualifications held, about 45–50 (if not already a graduate more years of study are involved to get a degree, therefore entry into the profession would be deferred)

6. Minimum education standards necessary

First degree or postgraduate qualification in library and information science accredited by the Library Association is usually the minimum requirement for professional posts in the UK. Most practising professional librarians and information officers also gain Chartered Membership of the Library Association

7. Qualifying examinations

8. Essential experience

Usually postgraduate students are required to have obtained about a year's pre-course non-professional experience in a library or information environment. No pre-course experience is required of undergraduates

9. Desirable experience

10. Training available (course(s) and examples of existing providers)

   (a) Full-time

First degrees and postgraduate qualifications accredited by the Association are offered by a number of institutions in the UK. A list is available from the Association. Write to the Education Department of the Library Association for their careers leaflets and 'Where to study in the UK'

   (b) Part-time

   (c) Correspondence course

Post-experience MLib available from University College of Wales, Aberystwyth. Graduate level applicants with substantial information work experience may be considered

   (d) Distance learning

   (e) Other

11. Additional comments (government grants and other initiatives for mature students, bursaries, etc)

There is a paucity of finance for full-time postgraduate students. Students over 40 are not eligible for postgraduate bursaries in any event. Undergraduate students may be eligible for mandatory grants for full-time study from their local education authority. Many mature students study part-time, often with support from their employers, in the library and information field. Such support must be negotiated on an individual basis by students with their employers

Job dimensions: Librarian/Information Officer

Key: HD – Highly Descriptive, D – Descriptive, = In the middle

		HD	D	=	D	HD	
1.	Supervise many	X				X	No supervision
2.	Teamwork	X					Work independently
3.	Customer contact	X					No customer contact
4.	Work in large organisation		X		X		Work alone
5.	Produce goods				X		Provide a service
6.	Fixed salary	X					Paid by results
7.	Flexitime	X					Fixed hours
8.	Routine work		X			X	Lots of surprises
9.	Lots of travel		X			X	No travel
10.	Closely managed		X				Managed from afar
11.	Work with same group	X			X		Work with different people
12.	Work indoors	X					Work outside
13.	Highly technical	X					Not technical
14.	Little innovation					X	Considerable innovation
15.	Short work cycles		X		X		Long work projects
16.	Low financial risk		X				High financial risk
17.	High attention to detail	X					Low attention to detail
18.	High specialisation		X		X		Low specialisation
19.	High visibility	X					Low visibility
20.	Extended working hours	X				X	9–5 job
21.	Many deadlines		X				Few deadlines
22.	Others depend on you	X					Little dependence
23.	Highly structured		X				Little structure
		HD	D	=	D	HD	

Local Government

Local government is one of Britain's largest employers. Over 2½ million people work in 449 local authorities in England and Wales. There is a great range of opportunities.

Local government is about the management of a wide variety of important local services by elected local authorities. To many people local government may conjure up an image of office work, but a broad range of services is provided and the scale of operation means there is scope for a wide variety of occupations. As with any other industry, the qualifications and skills you need depend on the types of post available. There are often vacancies for a multiplicity of jobs that may not require any previous qualifications or training. You learn on the job with training available as you progress. The training and development of staff has always been a high priority for local authorities. Most people are given release for qualification training as well as training while doing the job.

The list below will give you an idea of the range of careers and jobs in local government:

- *Professional staff:* local government is a major employer of many professional staff; for example, engineers, surveyors, planners, accountants, solicitors, librarians and computer specialists. It is the major employer in some other professions such as environmental health officers and town planners.
- *Technical staff:* for example, architectural technicians, engineering technicians, library assistants and legal executives where special training or expertise is required.
- *Administrative and clerical staff:* concerned with putting into effect decisions made by a local authority and helping the professional and technical staff to do their jobs.
- *Craft and manual work:* where there is a wide range of opportunities, for example in the building trades, catering, gardening, home help services, care assistants, vehicle maintenance and road works.

You can contact the personnel officer of your local authority or the authority in the area where you would like to work. He or she may be able to send you a list of current vacancies or give you advice. You can find the addresses in your local telephone directory. Alternatively, the addresses of all local authorities can be found in the *Municipal Year Book*, which is available in the reference section of most public libraries. See also CATLOG, the handbook of Careers and Training in Local Government.

Local authorities are encouraged to advertise their jobs widely in order to attract the best candidates. You will find these advertisements in:

- your local newspaper;
- national daily and Sunday newspapers;
- *Opportunities*, a weekly publication which should be in your local library;
- a whole range of specialist journals, many of which may also be found in your local library – *Local Government Chronicle, Municipal Journal, Surveyor*, and *Community Care and Education* are well-known examples.

There is no central recruitment agency for local authorities nor do they adopt a standard approach in recruiting staff. While some have a recruitment and training programme, others recruit only as and when they have vacancies.

Careers leaflets

An extensive range of careers leaflets is available from Local Government Opportunities, Local Government Management Board, Arndale House, Arndale Centre, Luton, Beds LU1 2TS; Tel: 0582 451166. These include Accountants and Accounting Technicians; Administration and Clerical Work; Architects and Architectural Technicians; Careers Officers; Engineering; Environmental Health Officers; Housing Managers; Information Management; Introduction to Local Government; Leisure and Recreation Management; Library and Information Work; Personnel and Training; Planners and Planning Technicians; Public Relations; Social Workers and Carers; Solicitors and Legal Executives; Surveyors and Surveying Technicians; Trading Standards Officers; Working with Children; Community Workers; Crafts; Economic Development Officers; Valuers.

The above information applies to England and Wales. Readers in Scotland and Northern Ireland should raise any queries with their local authorities, although the Local Government Management Board will respond if possible.

Two career switches: From local government to charity work to university lecturer – how bad news led to a satisfying career

Paul enjoyed a career spanning nearly 37 years in local government. He worked in his own time to obtain a degree in law and to qualify as a chartered secretary, which led eventually to an appointment as deputy clerk of a large urban district council. Paul thought he had a secure job and the prospect of

Job dimensions: Local Government Administrative Officer

Key: HD – Highly Descriptive, D – Descriptive, = In the middle

		HD	D	=	D	HD	
1.	Supervise many		X				No supervision
2.	Teamwork		X				Work independently
3.	Customer contact			X			No customer contact
4.	Work in large organisation		X				Work alone
5.	Produce goods				X		Provide a service
6.	Fixed salary	X					Paid by results
7.	Flexitime	X		X			Fixed hours
8.	Routine work		X				Lots of surprises
9.	Lots of travel					X	No travel
10.	Closely managed	X					Managed from afar
11.	Work with same group	X					Work with different people
12.	Work indoors	X					Work outside
13.	Highly technical				X		Not technical
14.	Little innovation	X					Considerable innovation
15.	Short work cycles			X			Long work projects
16.	Low financial risk	X					High financial risk
17.	High attention to detail		X				Low attention to detail
18.	High specialisation			X			Low specialisation
19.	High visibility			X			Low visibility
20.	Extended working hours					X	9–5 job
21.	Many deadlines		X				Few deadlines
22.	Others depend on you		X				Little dependence
23.	Highly structured	X					Little structure
		HD	D	=	D	HD	

Questionnaire: Environmental Health

1. Name and address of organisation	The Institution of Environmental Health Officers, 16 Great Guildford Street, London SE1 0ES
2. Telephone no	071-928 6006
3. Fax no	071-928 6953
4. Typically, for what job(s) does membership of your organisation qualify a person?	Environmental Health Officer
5. Up to what age is it practical for our readers to consider a career change to these occupations?	45 years
6. Minimum education standards necessary	Two A levels (including one science) plus five O levels (including English, mathematics plus two sciences)
7. Qualifying examinations	Diploma or degree in environmental health or postgraduate qualification (from accredited college/polytechnic/university)
8. Training available (course(s) and examples of existing providers)	
(a) Full-time	All colleges except University College, Salford
(b) Part-time	University College, Salford
(c) Correspondence course	—
(d) Distance learning	—
(e) Other	—
9. Additional comments (government grants and other initiatives for mature students, bursaries, etc)	Send for the brochure 'A Career in Environmental Health'. This covers the various aspects of the Environmental Health Officer's duties. These duties can include food safety and hygiene, working environment, pollution, noise, housing, pest control, communicable diseases, and water and waste. The brochure also outlines the routes to take to qualify, and lists the colleges offering courses

Job dimensions: Environmental Health Officer

Key: HD – Highly Descriptive, D – Descriptive, = In the middle

		HD	D	=	D	HD	
1.	Supervise many				X		No supervision
2.	Teamwork	X					Work independently
3.	Customer contact	X					No customer contact
4.	Work in large organisation		X——X				Work alone
5.	Produce goods					X	Provide a service
6.	Fixed salary	X					Paid by results
7.	Flexitime			X——X			Fixed hours
8.	Routine work		X——X				Lots of surprises
9.	Lots of travel		X——X				No travel
10.	Closely managed	X					Managed from afar
11.	Work with same group	X					Work with different people
12.	Work indoors		X——X				Work outside
13.	Highly technical	X					Not technical
14.	Little innovation				X		Considerable innovation
15.	Short work cycles		X				Long work projects
16.	Low financial risk		X				High financial risk
17.	High attention to detail	X					Low attention to detail
18.	High specialisation		X				Low specialisation
19.	High visibility		X				Low visibility
20.	Extended working hours			X——X			9–5 job
21.	Many deadlines		X				Few deadlines
22.	Others depend on you	X					Little dependence
23.	Highly structured		X				Little structure
		HD	D	=	D	HD	

possible succession to the top job as clerk of the council.

Then, in 1974, the general reorganisation of local government saw the amalgamation of his authority with the adjoining larger borough council and the disappearance of his 'secure' job. Paul took the option to retire at the early age of 52. In the run-up to the change, he applied for an appointment as general secretary of a national charity. His experience in management and administration secured him the appointment and he embarked on a new career.

Together with the director of the charity, he became joint author of a successful book dealing with their special field of interest. Some three years later, he gave up his appointment to become a freelance lecturer and continued his collaboration with his co-author to write a further three books.

He subsequently became an associate lecturer at a university, a post he held until normal retirement age, and he is still active in his chosen field.

Paul comments that he thought he had a secure job in local government until normal retirement age. But the loss of that gave him the opportunity for a new and satisfying career. He feels that for him, at any rate, the 1974 reorganisation of local government was a blessing in disguise.

The National Health Service

The National Health Service is one of the largest organisations in Europe, employing nearly 1 million people in a wide range of jobs. All these occupations are related to health care, but the sheer variety and number of professions might surprise you. A large hospital is virtually a self-contained community demanding round-the-clock provision of a range of services.

A broadsheet entitled 'Health Service Careers' is available, and lists 50 different careers and professions. You can obtain copies of this and other Health Service careers literature from the address on page 71. For each type of post, the educational and age requirements, training and qualifications are listed, together with an address for further information. This may not be your local hospital. Certain technical vacancies may exist only in specialist or teaching hospitals. Posts which come under the umbrella of community care are likely to involve visiting patients in their own homes. The list of careers, apart from the obvious medical staff, makes a fascinating mixture.

Art, Drama and Music Therapist
Audio-visual Technician
Computing Staff
Dietician

Dental Support Staff
Medical Laboratory Staff
Orthoptist
Physiological Measurement Technician
Physiotherapist
Radiographer
Stores Staff.

In the current employment climate, many hospital personnel officers are prepared to be flexible when recruiting staff. They are willing to consider job-sharing and part-time work for many of the Service's professional and support staff. Many hospitals, particularly in areas of high employment, will consider applicants up to 65 years of age. The provision of crèches is being examined urgently as a means of recruiting and retaining staff. Since April 1990 nurseries and playgroups provided by employers are tax-free for employees. Some hospitals operate a play scheme for older children (5 to 12 years) during school holidays.

The Health Minister recently announced that National Health Service employees will be able to take (unpaid) career breaks of up to five years. The aim is to keep staff who want to leave temporarily to start a family or to care for relatives.

Services such as finance, personnel, supplies and planning are vital to general management. During employment, medical and administrative opportunities may exist after two to three years of training for professional qualifications. People returning to work, without professional or formal qualifications but with general experience, can apply for posts in many areas such as health care assistance, patient services, general administration or 'hotel services'. People with administrative skills are often required in the patient services sector.

To find out more about careers in the Health Service, contact the personnel officer at your local hospital or write for leaflets, posters and broadsheets to: Health Service Careers, PO Box 204, London SE5 7ES.

In view of the size of the NHS and the interest shown in the variety of careers, a selection of questionnaires completed by the Society of Chiropodists, the College of Radiographers (with case histories), the College of Speech Therapists, the College of Occupational Therapists and the Chartered Society of Physiotherapy are included in the following pages Bursaries may be available to train as a radiographer or occupational therapist. If you have a music degree and would like to put something back into the community, you might consider taking a music therapy course (see page 75). The British Society for Music Therapy was founded to promote the use and development of music therapy in the treatment, education, rehabilitation and training of children and adults suffering from emotional, physical or mental handicap.

Chiropody/Podiatry

The care of the feet as a part of medical practice is as old as medicine itself. Chiropody attained full professional status in 1960. Chiropodists practise in the NHS, in private surgeries and in industry.

The three-year course of the Society of Chiropodists is both theoretical and practical, and now leads to a BSc degree in most of the recognised schools. In the questionnaire completed by the Society of Chiropodists, it was stated that there were no minimum educational standards for mature students who were accepted by the Head of School. Let us enlarge on this aspect. Mature students have to show ability, and a science-based background is useful. Several of the schools have Access-type courses, part-time but very concentrated, for the year prior to commencement for mature students. Those making a career change after service in the police, nursing or the forces will find their experience useful.

Only half the estimated current demand for chiropody services can be met. Many sufferers either receive no treatment or treatment too infrequently to prevent deterioration of their foot problem. Some state registered chiropodists work within the National Health Service. Those considering chiropody are reminded that, to work within the NHS, state registration is the only chiropodial qualification accepted. Chiropody treatment is free within the NHS to 'priority' groups.

Many state registered chiropodists, probably about half those currently practising, are self-employed, with their own surgeries or visiting practices. Anyone may attend their surgeries (without referral by a doctor).

The registered profession is gradually turning to podiatry as a title.

Questionnaire: Chiropody/Podiatry

1. Name and address of organisation

   The Society of Chiropodists, 53 Welbeck Street, London W1M 7HE

2. Telephone no

   071-486 3381

3. Fax no

   071-935 6359

4. Typically, for what job(s) does membership of your organisation qualify a person?

   All levels of chiropodial care, from simple conservative treatment to surgical procedures on the feet. This may be within the National Health Service, in industry or in private practice

5. Up to what age is it practical for our readers to consider a career change to these occupations?

   Mature students are accepted up to a probable maximum of 50 years. Such students are accepted by interview with individual Heads of School

6. Minimum education standards necessary

   Nil for mature students accepted by Head of School, but see page 72.

7. Examinations necessary to qualify as a state registered chiropodist

   A three-year BSc degree course or, in a few schools, a diploma equivalent

8. Essential experience

   —

9. Desirable experience

   Work with people/work in sciences, especially biological

10. Training available (course(s) and examples of existing providers)

    Fifteen recognised schools of chiropody. One is in the NHS (the London Foot Hospital). The others are in colleges of higher education, in polytechnics or in universities

    (a) Full-time

    (b) Part-time

    —

    (c) Correspondence course

    Not to lead to state registration and acceptance by Department of Health and NHS

    (d) Distance learning

    Only for postgraduate work

    (e) Other

    Plenty of postgraduate courses at all levels from refresher to bone surgery courses and a BSc (Hons)

11. Additional comments (government grants and other initiatives for mature students, bursaries, etc)

    Before the advent of our first degrees, grants were discretionary. Now they may be mandatory, depending on the individual. Some health authorities provide sponsorship. Most qualifying students want employment within the NHS, and only state registration allows this. Only the education offered through the Society of Chiropodists' schools leads to registration. Send for leaflet 'The Profession of Chiropody'

Job dimensions: Chiropodist/Podiatrist

Key: HD – Highly Descriptive, D – Descriptive, = In the middle

		HD	D	=	D	HD	
1.	Supervise many				X		No supervision
2.	Teamwork				X		Work independently
3.	Customer contact	X					No customer contact
4.	Work in large organisation				X		Work alone
5.	Produce goods					X	Provide a service
6.	Fixed salary			X			Paid by results
7.	Flexitime					X	Fixed hours
8.	Routine work			X			Lots of surprises
9.	Lots of travel			X			No travel
10.	Closely managed			X			Managed from afar
11.	Work with same group					X	Work with different people
12.	Work indoors	X					Work outside
13.	Highly technical		X				Not technical
14.	Little innovation			X			Considerable innovation
15.	Short work cycles	X					Long work projects
16.	Low financial risk			X			High financial risk
17.	High attention to detail		X				Low attention to detail
18.	High specialisation			X			Low specialisation
19.	High visibility	X					Low visibility
20.	Extended working hours					X	9–5 job
21.	Many deadlines					X	Few deadlines
22.	Others depend on you	X					Little dependence
23.	Highly structured				X		Little structure
		HD	D	=	D	HD	

Note. There is a fixed salary in the NHS. A fee structure applies if self-employed.

Questionnaire: Music Therapy

1. Name and address of organisation

   British Society for Music Therapy, 69 Avondale Avenue, East Barnet, Herts EN4 8NB

2. Telephone no

   081-368 8879

3. Fax no

   —

4. Typically, for what job(s) does membership of your organisation qualify a person?

   None. The Society's membership is open to *all* interested in music therapy

5. Up to what age is it practical for our readers to consider a career change to these occupations?

   No age limit

6. Minimum education standards necessary

   Usually a music degree before a music therapy course

7. Qualifying examinations

   Music degree

8. Essential experience

   —

9. Desirable experience

   Knowing something about disabilities – experience in a care situation

10. Training available (course(s) and examples of existing providers)

    (a) Full-time

    Three in London

    (b) Part-time

    —

    (c) Correspondence course

    —

    (d) Distance learning

    —

    (e) Other

    —

11. Additional comments (government grants and other initiatives for mature students, bursaries, etc)

    The authors add: This society is not a professional body. Music therapy is now an established profession, and therapists are employed in a wide range of hospitals, special schools and community settings. Those interested in a career in music therapy should write to the Association of Professional Music Therapists' Administrator, 68 Pierce Lane, Fulbourn, Cambs CB1 5DL

Job dimensions: Music Therapist

Key: HD – Highly Descriptive, D – Descriptive, = In the middle

	HD	D	=	D	HD	
1. Supervise many				X		No supervision
2. Teamwork		X				Work independently
3. Customer contact	X					No customer contact
4. Work in large organisation				X		Work alone
5. Produce goods				X		Provide a service
6. Fixed salary	X					Paid by results
7. Flexitime				X—X		Fixed hours
8. Routine work			X			Lots of surprises
9. Lots of travel				X		No travel
10. Closely managed			X———	X		Managed from afar
11. Work with same group				X		Work with different people
12. Work indoors	X					Work outside
13. Highly technical	X					Not technical
14. Little innovation				X		Considerable innovation
15. Short work cycles		X———	X			Long work projects
16. Low financial risk	X					High financial risk
17. High attention to detail		X				Low attention to detail
18. High specialisation		X				Low specialisation
19. High visibility	X					Low visibility
20. Extended working hours				X—X		9–5 job
21. Many deadlines				X		Few deadlines
22. Others depend on you	X					Little dependence
23. Highly structured				X		Little structure
	HD	D	=	D	HD	

Questionnaire: Occupational Therapy

1. Name and address of organisation	The College of Occupational Therapists, 6–8 Marshalsea Road, London SE1 1HL
2. Telephone no	071-357 6480
3. Fax no	071-378 8095
4. Typically, for what job(s) does membership of your organisation qualify a person?	Occupational therapists and occupational therapy helpers/assistants in the Health Service, Social Services Department, occupational therapists in private practice and those employed as occupational therapists or helpers/assistants in charitable/voluntary organisations
5. Up to what age is it practical for our readers to consider a career change to these occupations?	Mid to late 40s
6. Minimum education standards necessary	The most widely exercised criterion for the selection of mature candidates is that they show evidence of recent academic study – preferably to A-level standard, ie an A level, OU credit or a validated access course
7. Qualifying examinations	Diploma or degree in Occupational Therapy
8. Essential experience	It is expected that candidates will have visited a range of occupational therapy departments prior to being interviewed for a place, to demonstrate they have a clear understanding of the roles and functions of an occupational therapist
9. Desirable experience	General life experience can be used because of the diversity of an occupational therapist's role; work experience with the physically or mentally impaired or elderly people is an advantage
10. Training available (course(s) and examples of existing providers)	
(a) Full-time	Degree in occupational therapy or an accelerated two-year diploma course for graduates
(b) Part-time	In-service diploma course available to those already employed as occupational therapy helpers or assistants
(c) Correspondence course	—
(d) Distance learning	—
(e) Other	—
11. Additional comments (government grants and other initiatives for mature students, bursaries, etc)	Regional Health Authority bursaries are awarded on attainment of a place on a full-time degree course. Some health authorities and social services may offer sponsorship if sought by the candidate. In-service course fees are negotiated with the employer

77

Job dimensions: Occupational Therapist

Key: HD – Highly Descriptive, D – Descriptive, = In the middle

		HD	D	=	D	HD	
1.	Supervise many				X		No supervision
2.	Teamwork		X				Work independently
3.	Customer contact	X					No customer contact
4.	Work in large organisation			X			Work alone
5.	Produce goods					X	Provide a service
6.	Fixed salary	X					Paid by results
7.	Flexitime					X	Fixed hours
8.	Routine work			X			Lots of surprises
9.	Lots of travel				X—X		No travel
10.	Closely managed			X			Managed from afar
11.	Work with same group			X—X			Work with different people
12.	Work indoors	X					Work outside
13.	Highly technical			X			Not technical
14.	Little innovation			X			Considerable innovation
15.	Short work cycles		X————X				Long work projects
16.	Low financial risk	X					High financial risk
17.	High attention to detail				X		Low attention to detail
18.	High specialisation		X				Low specialisation
19.	High visibility	X					Low visibility
20.	Extended working hours				X—X		9–5 job
21.	Many deadlines				X		Few deadlines
22.	Others depend on you	X					Little dependence
23.	Highly structured			X			Little structure
		HD	D	=	D	HD	

Questionnaire: Physiotherapy

1. Name and address of organisation

   Chartered Society of Physiotherapy, 14 Bedford Row, London WC1R 4ED

2. Telephone no

   071-242 1941

3. Fax no

   071-831 4509

4. Typically, for what job(s) does membership of your organisation qualify a person?

   Chartered physiotherapist. (The trend is towards specialisation. There is tremendous scope in a number of areas, eg manipulation, sports injuries, teaching or private practice.)

5. Up to what age is it practical for our readers to consider a career change to these occupations?

   35

6. Minimum education standards necessary

   Five GCSEs and two A levels

7. Qualifying examinations

   BSc in Physiotherapy

8. Essential experience

   —

9. Desirable experience

   You need to be a good communicator, patient and caring

10. Training available (course(s) and examples of existing providers)

    (a) Full-time

    Usually a three-year course

    (b) Part-time

    —

    (c) Correspondence course

    —

    (d) Distance learning

    —

    (e) Other

    —

11. Additional comments (government grants and other initiatives for mature students, bursaries, etc)

    Applications are welcome from mature people who can show evidence of recent successful academic study. Write for guidelines for mature applicants and leaflets of recognised schools

Job dimensions: Physiotherapist

Key: HD – Highly Descriptive, D – Descriptive, = In the middle

		HD	D	=	D	HD	
1.	Supervise many				X		No supervision
2.	Teamwork		X—		—X		Work independently
3.	Customer contact	X					No customer contact
4.	Work in large organisation		X—		—X		Work alone
5.	Produce goods					X	Provide a service
6.	Fixed salary	X—			—X		Paid by results
7.	Flexitime					X	Fixed hours
8.	Routine work		X—		—X		Lots of surprises
9.	Lots of travel				X		No travel
10.	Closely managed			X			Managed from afar
11.	Work with same group		X				Work with different people
12.	Work indoors		X				Work outside
13.	Highly technical	X					Not technical
14.	Little innovation			X			Considerable innovation
15.	Short work cycles	X—				—X	Long work projects
16.	Low financial risk	X					High financial risk
17.	High attention to detail	X					Low attention to detail
18.	High specialisation		X				Low specialisation
19.	High visibility	X					Low visibility
20.	Extended working hours				X		9–5 job
21.	Many deadlines				X		Few deadlines
22.	Others depend on you	X					Little dependence
23.	Highly structured		X				Little structure
		HD	D	=	D	HD	

Radiography

Radiography is a caring profession which calls for considerable technological expertise. There are two branches: diagnostic radiography and therapeutic radiography. Diagnostic radiographers are responsible for producing high-quality images on film and other recording materials which help doctors to diagnose disease and the extent of injuries. Therapeutic radiographers help to treat patients, many of whom have cancer, using ionising radiation and other techniques.

Personal qualities

As well as having an interest in science, you have to be a caring and compassionate person, sufficiently level-headed not to be upset when dealing with sick people. You have to be patient and calm when faced with people who may be frightened or are being difficult. Your health must be good and you have to be reasonably strong, because you may have to help lift people and move heavy equipment.

Career prospects

Almost every hospital has some form of diagnostic X-ray equipment, whereas radiotherapy tends to be carried out in regional centres, so there are many more diagnostic radiographer posts.

You will be able to train further and specialise in, say, medical ultrasound or radionuclide imaging.

Once you have gained experience, there will be chances of promotion to senior, superintendent and teaching posts. Some combine teaching with clinical work. Promotion to a top post can come quite early, but you will first have to obtain higher qualifications. From 1992 all qualifying courses in the UK will be degree courses.

Two case histories

Christopher has been qualified for three years and is a diagnostic radiographer at a large teaching hospital. 'This morning, I started on the wards, X-raying two patients who have had heart bypass grafts and have just come off intensive care. Then in the recovery room, I X-rayed the chest of a patient who wasn't coming round very well from the anaesthestic. We often work in operating theatres. For instance, we take films when a patient is having a gall bladder removed.

'We weren't too busy in theatre today so I helped out in one of the general rooms where I radiographed an old lady's fractured femur. After that I went into the fluoroscopy suite to take films during an investigation of the kidneys. Then we prepared the room for a barium swallow and explained the procedure to the patient. Once a patient has drunk the barium mixture given by the radiologist, we take films at various stages.'

Normally, radiographers work from nine to five, but they also have some 'on-call' work at night and are expected to cover the weekends by rotation. 'I like being alone at night when the buck stops with you. It is your responsibility to decide which patient needs to be dealt with first. You can be working solidly all night, with perhaps ten minutes for supper, and then not be able to sit down again until two or three in the morning.'

Though it is hard work, Christopher enjoys it enormously. 'You are travelling throughout the hospital, not just based in one department. You meet a lot of people and must remember that you are an ambassador for your department. A large part of any kind of clinical work is diplomacy.'

Mary is qualified in both diagnostic and therapeutic radiography and is a therapeutic radiographer at a large teaching hospital. Therapy radiographers treat people with cancer and non-malignant diseases.

'The main reason I chose therapy is that I get to know my patients really well because they attend frequently. A lot of our work consists of looking after them and making sure they get the help they need. We warn them about possible side-effects of treatment, see that they take the right drugs and perhaps advise on diet. Sometimes we have to sort out transport for them or arrange for them to see social workers.'

The planning procedure is very important. It is a team effort, in which radiographers work with doctors, physicists and nursing staff. The aim is to determine the correct dose of radiation, decide where the beam should enter and exit, and which structures should be treated and which avoided. The location of a tumour and its size are discovered with the aid of computerised tomography (CT) or magnetic resonance scans or other diagnostic procedures. 'You place the patient precisely in the treatment position and then simulate the treatment and take an X-ray image of the area to be treated. We can then localise the tumour before the start of therapy.'

Therapeutic radiographers are likely to work more regular hours than diagnostic radiographers, though it is necessary to have some 'out of hours' cover for specific treatment. The atmosphere in a treatment unit is a hopeful one. About 60 per cent of those who come for radiotherapy can be cured.

'Many of the people who come to us are still fit and don't look ill. We do, of course, get some patients who are very sick, but in those circumstances we are relieving pain, and their low spirits improve. There is terrific job satisfaction. It's marvellous when people come back years later and are hardly

Questionnaire: Radiography

1. Name and address of organisation

   The College of Radiographers, 14 Upper Wimpole Street, London W1M 8BN

2. Telephone no

   071-935 5726

3. Fax no

   071-487 3483

4. Typically, for what job(s) does membership of your organisation qualify a person?

   Radiographer

5. Up to what age is it practical for our readers to consider a career change to these occupations?

   No upper age limit

6. Minimum education standards necessary

   Mature entry is possible without formal educational qualifications

7. Qualifying examinations

   BSc in Radiography

8. Essential experience

9. Desirable experience

   } All appropriate experience is considered

10. Training available (course(s) and examples of existing providers)

    (a) Full-time   Yes

    (b) Part-time   —

    (c) Correspondence course   —

    (d) Distance learning   —

    (e) Other   —

11. Additional comments (government grants and other initiatives for mature students, bursaries, etc)

    As the course is a degree course it qualifies for a mandatory LEA award throughout the UK. Additionally, in England and Wales, Department of Health bursaries are alternatively available and previous educational awards would not normally count against applicants for such bursaries

83

Job dimensions: Radiographer

Key: HD – Highly Descriptive,   D – Descriptive,   = In the middle

		HD	D	=	D	HD	
1.	Supervise many				X		No supervision
2.	Teamwork	X					Work independently
3.	Customer contact	X					No customer contact
4.	Work in large organisation			X			Work alone
5.	Produce goods					X	Provide a service
6.	Fixed salary	X					Paid by results
7.	Flexitime				X		Fixed hours
8.	Routine work		X				Lots of surprises
9.	Lots of travel					X	No travel
10.	Closely managed		X				Managed from afar
11.	Work with same group		X				Work with different people
12.	Work indoors	X					Work outside
13.	Highly technical			X			Not technical
14.	Little innovation	X					Considerable innovation
15.	Short work cycles	X					Long work projects
16.	Low financial risk	X					High financial risk
17.	High attention to detail		X				Low attention to detail
18.	High specialisation		X				Low specialisation
19.	High visibility	X					Low visibility
20.	Extended working hours					X	9–5 job
21.	Many deadlines				X		Few deadlines
22.	Others depend on you	X					Little dependence
23.	Highly structured		X				Little structure
		HD	D	=	D	HD	

recognisable because they look so well. Most of them come to the department and say, '"Hi! I thought I would let you know how I am getting on." At Christmas they send us cards.'

The questionnaire completed by the College of Radiographers appears on page 83. Radiography *welcomes mature entry students* who may lack formal qualifications. For students who feel that they do not have the necessary confidence to enter training, access courses can be arranged.

A leaflet on radiography as a career, a list of education centres and details of pay scales can be obtained from the College of Radiographers.

Questionnaire: Speech Therapy

1. Name and address of organisation

   The College of Speech and Language Therapists, 7 Bath Place, Rivington Street, London EC2A 3DR

2. Telephone no

   071-613 3855

3. Fax no

   071-613 3854

4. Typically, for what job(s) does membership of your organisation qualify a person?

   Speech and language therapist – clinical practitioner – educationalist – manager

5. Up to what age is it practical for our readers to consider a career change to these occupations?

   50

6. Minimum education standards necessary

   A level or indication of recent academic activity at this level

7. Qualifying examinations

   Degree/postgraduate diploma

8. Essential experience

   Ability to relate to people

9. Desirable experience

   Recent academic activity

10. Training available (course(s) and examples of existing providers)

    (a) Full-time

    Fifteen degree courses and several postgraduate courses

    (b) Part-time

    —

    (c) Correspondence course

    —

    (d) Distance learning

    —

    (e) Other

    —

11. Additional comments (government grants and other initiatives for mature students, bursaries, etc)

    The normal LEA grant system applies; NHS bursaries available only rarely

Job dimensions: Speech Therapist

Key: HD – Highly Descriptive, D – Descriptive, = In the middle

		HD	D	=	D	HD	
1.	Supervise many				X		No supervision
2.	Teamwork		X				Work independently
3.	Customer contact	X					No customer contact
4.	Work in large organisation			X			Work alone
5.	Produce goods					X	Provide a service
6.	Fixed salary	X					Paid by results
7.	Flexitime					X	Fixed hours
8.	Routine work		X				Lots of surprises
9.	Lots of travel					X	No travel
10.	Closely managed			X			Managed from afar
11.	Work with same group				X		Work with different people
12.	Work indoors	X					Work outside
13.	Highly technical		X				Not technical
14.	Little innovation			X			Considerable innovation
15.	Short work cycles		X		X		Long work projects
16.	Low financial risk	X					High financial risk
17.	High attention to detail		X				Low attention to detail
18.	High specialisation		X				Low specialisation
19.	High visibility	X					Low visibility
20.	Extended working hours					X	9–5 job
21.	Many deadlines					X	Few deadlines
22.	Others depend on you	X					Little dependence
23.	Highly structured		X				Little structure
		HD	D	=	D	HD	

Questionnaire: Optician

1. Name and address of organisation

Association of British Dispensing Opticians (ABDO), 6 Hurlingham Business Park, Sulivan Road, London SW6 3DU

2. Telephone no

071-736 0088

3. Fax no

071-731 5531

4. Typically, for what job(s) does membership of your organisation qualify a person?

A dispensing optician converts a prescription into a pair of spectacles and, if qualified, contact lenses, discussing with the patient the relevant frame type and lenses, bearing in mind the patient's work and leisure activities

5. Up to what age is it practical for our readers to consider a career change to these occupations?

The upper age limit is generally governed by the student's ability to study. There is no age limit on entry

6. Minimum education standards necessary

Five GCSE/GCE passes to include English, mathematics or physics, a third science-based subject and two other subjects; all must be at grade A, B or C

7. Qualifying examinations

FBDO (Fellowship of the Association of British Dispensing Opticians)

8. Essential experience

Face-to-face contact with the public. Marketing and sales

9. Desirable experience

Some experience of working in an optical practice

10. Training available (course(s) and examples of existing providers)

Bradford, City and Glasgow Colleges undertake day-release training and the Association runs a correspondence course

   (a) Full-time
   (b) Part-time
   (c) Correspondence course
   (d) Distance learning

Yes

   (e) Other

—

11. Additional comments (government grants and other initiatives for mature students, bursaries, etc)

Students interested in full-time education should contact their local education authority to ascertain whether they will be eligible for a local authority grant

Job dimensions: Optician

Key: HD – Highly Descriptive, D – Descriptive, = In the middle

		HD	D	=	D	HD	
1.	Supervise many			X			No supervision
2.	Teamwork		X				Work independently
3.	Customer contact	X					No customer contact
4.	Work in large organisation				X		Work alone
5.	Produce goods					X	Provide a service
6.	Fixed salary	X					Paid by results
7.	Flexitime				X		Fixed hours
8.	Routine work	X					Lots of surprises
9.	Lots of travel					X	No travel
10.	Closely managed				X		Managed from afar
11.	Work with same group					X	Work with different people
12.	Work indoors	X					Work outside
13.	Highly technical	X					Not technical
14.	Little innovation		X				Considerable innovation
15.	Short work cycles	X					Long work projects
16.	Low financial risk	X					High financial risk
17.	High attention to detail	X					Low attention to detail
18.	High specialisation		X				Low specialisation
19.	High visibility	X					Low visibility
20.	Extended working hours					X	9–5 job
21.	Many deadlines			X——X			Few deadlines
22.	Others depend on you		X				Little dependence
23.	Highly structured		X				Little structure
		HD	D	=	D	HD	

Religion – Christianity

A Ministry in the Church
All Christian churches welcome mature candidates but there is insufficient space here to cover all the major Christian churches in detail. Talk things over with your local priest or minister if you would like further information. Church of England details are on page 91. The headquarters of the major denominations are as follows:

Baptist Union, Ministry Office, Baptist Union of Great Britain, Baptist House, 129 The Broadway, Didcot, Oxon OX11 8RT

Church of Scotland, Department of Education, Church of Scotland Office, 121 George Street, Edinburgh EH2 4YN

Methodist Church, Division of Ministries, 25 Marylebone Road, London NW1 5JR

Roman Catholic Church, National Religious Vocations Centre, 31 Moor Road, Headingley, Leeds LS6 4BG

The Salvation Army National Headquarters, 101 Queen Victoria Street, London EC4P 4EP

United Reformed Church, Ministries Department, 86 Tavistock Place, London WC1H 9RT

Other religions

The Multi-Faith Centre
Readers interested in other religions may wish to contact the Multi-Faith Centre. It is a registered charitable company and its directors represent the Hindu, Muslim, Sikh, Buddhist, Jewish and Christian traditions. The Centre is affiliated to Selly Oak College, Birmingham.

The Centre's aim is to provide 'Education by Encounter' through a permanent team of multi-faith, multi-cultural educators from the various communities. For details send an SAE to the Network Contact, Executive Director, Harborne Hall, Old Church Road, Harborne, Birmingham B17 0BD; 021-427 1044.

Questionnaire: Religion – Christianity

1. Name and address of organisation	The Vocations Officer, Advisory Board of Ministry (C of E), Church House, Great Smith Street, London SW1P 3NZ
2. Telephone no	071-222 9011
3. Fax no	071-799 2714
4. Typically, for what job(s) does membership of your organisation qualify a person?	The Advisory Board is concerned with the recruitment, selection and training of candidates for the priesthood, the diaconate, and the accredited lay ministry
5. Up to what age is it practical for our readers to consider a career change to these occupations?	Fifty is the usual age limit for candidates for stipendiary ministry
6. Minimum education standards necessary	No absolute standard is laid down for candidates over 25
7. Qualifying examinations	General Ministerial Examination (or other approved equivalents)
8. Essential experience	Membership of the Church of England through baptism and confirmation
9. Desirable experience	Pastoral
10. Training available (course(s) and examples of existing providers)	
(a) Full-time	Yes
(b) Part-time	
(c) Correspondence course	—
(d) Distance learning	Yes
(e) Other	—
11. Additional comments (government grants and other initiatives for mature students, bursaries, etc)	All recommended candidates are eligible for a grant from central church funds

Social Work

Social workers are a professional group employed mainly by local authorities but also by central government, and by voluntary and private organisations to provide personal social services. A social worker may be needed when people are sick or disabled; when they are under great stress, or in trouble with the law; or when their circumstances have created long-standing problems.

91

Job dimensions: Minister of the Church

Key: HD – Highly Descriptive,   D – Descriptive,   = In the middle

		HD	D	=	D	HD	
1.	Supervise many		X				No supervision
2.	Teamwork	X					Work independently
3.	Customer contact	X					No customer contact
4.	Work in large organisation			X			Work alone
5.	Produce goods					X	Provide a service
6.	Fixed salary	X					Paid by results
7.	Flexitime		X——X				Fixed hours
8.	Routine work		X——X				Lots of surprises
9.	Lots of travel			X			No travel
10.	Closely managed			X			Managed from afar
11.	Work with same group		X				Work with different people
12.	Work indoors		X				Work outside
13.	Highly technical				X		Not technical
14.	Little innovation		X				Considerable innovation
15.	Short work cycles			X—X			Long work projects
16.	Low financial risk	X					High financial risk
17.	High attention to detail				X		Low attention to detail
18.	High specialisation					X	Low specialisation
19.	High visibility	X					Low visibility
20.	Extended working hours		X——X				9–5 job
21.	Many deadlines		X				Few deadlines
22.	Others depend on you	X					Little dependence
23.	Highly structured		X				Little structure
		HD	D	=	D	HD	

To understand the problems of their clients, social workers must draw upon their own resources of care and understanding. They must have self-discipline, patience, persistence and the ability to help people face difficult situations.

Many social workers are based in offices in the areas where their clients live, meeting them at the office or in their homes. Others work in day centres, in offices near the courts, in residential homes or hostels, hospitals, health centres or group practices, child guidance clinics, day or boarding schools, or prisons.

Most social workers are employed by local authority social services departments (England and Wales) or social work departments (Scotland) or by area health and social services boards (Northern Ireland) or in education departments. Social workers are also employed as probation officers by probation committees (England and Wales) and by the Northern Ireland Probation Board. (See the Probation Service, page 58, and point 11. of the social work questionnaire on page 94.) In Scotland, the duties of probation officers are included in those of social workers employed by local authorities.

Employers throughout the UK recognise two currently available social work qualifications: the Certificate in Social Services (CSS) and the Certificate of Qualification in Social Work (CQSW). CSS students are normally employment-based – they keep their jobs (and remain at home) throughout the course. The CQSW is college-based. If already working, students have to give up their jobs. The Diploma in Social Work (DipSW) is a new award which will eventually replace the CSS and the CQSW after 1994/95, but both certificates will continue to be recognised as professional social work qualifications. To begin with, the DipSW will be either employment-based or college-based.

If you consider yourself a clear thinker and have plenty of energy – the work can be physically and emotionally tiring and the hours irregular – write to the CCETSW for their guides. *They will also send you details of any financial support available.* The leaflets spell out the types of career open to trained social workers. If you are undecided after studying the leaflets, take a job as an ancillary or assistant to a trained worker. You can then make your own career decision.

Questionnaire: Social Work

1. Name and address of organisation

   Central Council for Education and Training in Social Work (CCETSW), Derbyshire House, St Chad's Street, London WC1H 8AD (see also point 11)

2. Telephone no

   071-278 2455

3. Fax no

   071-278 2934

4. Typically, for what job(s) does membership of your organisation qualify a person?

   The social work profession

5. Up to what age is it practical for our readers to consider a career change to these occupations?

   People between 25 and 50 are advised to contact the course/programme organiser to discuss their applications

6. Minimum education standards necessary

   Applicants need to demonstrate their ability to study at higher education level. This is usually by some recent educational achievement

7. Qualifying examinations

   Students are assessed on practice placements. Other assessment varies from course to course and can include continuous assessment, essays or written examinations

8. Essential experience

   A minimum of one year's paid or voluntary work in a social work-related role is normally necessary

9. Desirable experience

   —

10. Training available (course(s) and examples of existing providers)

    (a) Full-time } Yes

    (b) Part-time

    (c) Correspondence course } Regulations allow for distance and open learning, though as yet no such course exists

    (d) Distance learning

11. Additional comments (government grants and other initiatives for mature students, bursaries, etc)

    Grants to cover fees and living expenses are discretionary awards from the local education authority on non-degree courses. Home Office sponsorship for people intending to work in the Probation Service is available. Courses are normally full time for two years and may be college- or work-based. Since 1991, more courses have followed a part-time route. Enrolment takes place in the autumn for courses commencing, in most cases, in the following year

Information from the CCETSW is also available from the following offices:

78–80 George Street, Edinburgh EH2 3BU; 031-220 0093

6 Malone Road, Belfast BT9 5BN; 0232 665390

St David's House, Wood Street, Cardiff CF1 1ES; 0222 226257

Job dimensions: Social Worker

Key: HD – Highly Descriptive, D – Descriptive, = In the middle

		HD	D	=	D	HD	
1.	Supervise many		X		X		No supervision
2.	Teamwork	X					Work independently
3.	Customer contact	X					No customer contact
4.	Work in large organisation			X			Work alone
5.	Produce goods				X		Provide a service
6.	Fixed salary	X					Paid by results
7.	Flexitime	X					Fixed hours
8.	Routine work				X		Lots of surprises
9.	Lots of travel		X		X		No travel
10.	Closely managed	X					Managed from afar
11.	Work with same group	X					Work with different people
12.	Work indoors		X		X		Work outside
13.	Highly technical		X				Not technical
14.	Little innovation					X	Considerable innovation
15.	Short work cycles	X				X	Long work projects
16.	Low financial risk				X		High financial risk
17.	High attention to detail	X					Low attention to detail
18.	High specialisation		X				Low specialisation
19.	High visibility	X					Low visibility
20.	Extended working hours		X		X		9–5 job
21.	Many deadlines		X				Few deadlines
22.	Others depend on you	X					Little dependence
23.	Highly structured	X					Little structure
		HD	D	=	D	HD	

95

B. Construction, Housing and Transport

Questionnaire: Architecture

1. Name and address of organisation — The Royal Institute of British Architects (RIBA), 66 Portland Place, London W1N 6EE

2. Telephone no — 071-580 5533

3. Fax no — 071-255 1541

4. Typically, for what job(s) does membership of your organisation qualify a person? — A wide variety of roles in the construction industry and beyond, particularly in the design field

5. Up to what age is it practical for our readers to consider a career change to these occupations? — Around 40 – it takes at least seven years to qualify (full time; longer for part time)

6. Minimum education standards necessary — Core GCSE, two or three academic A levels and portfolio, although mature entrants are treated individually

7. Qualifying examinations — The RIBA's own examinations or those of validated higher education institutions

8. Essential experience — Two years' minimum practical training is part of the qualification process

9. Desirable experience — —

10. Training available (course(s) and examples of existing providers)

    (a) Full-time — } Degree and Diploma in UFC* and PCFC* institutions

    (b) Part-time — }

    (c) Correspondence course — RIBA examinations in certain circumstances

    (d) Distance learning — Not possible yet to qualify this way, but packages are available to support learning

    (e) Other — —

11. Additional comments (government grants and other initiatives for mature students, bursaries, etc) — Five-year DES mandatory award but few sponsorships etc. There are some career opportunities within the profession for the enthusiast who does not wish to qualify. Vacancies may exist for architects' assistants, skilled draughtsmen and administrative staff. Write to the Institute for their leaflet 'A Career in Architecture'

    * The Universities Funding Council and the Polytechnics and Colleges Funding Council (formerly UGC and NAB)

Job dimensions: Architect

Key: HD – Highly Descriptive,   D – Descriptive,   = In the middle

		HD	D	=	D	HD	
1.	Supervise many		X—	—X			No supervision
2.	Teamwork		X				Work independently
3.	Customer contact		X				No customer contact
4.	Work in large organisation			X			Work alone
5.	Produce goods				X		Provide a service
6.	Fixed salary			X			Paid by results
7.	Flexitime			X			Fixed hours
8.	Routine work				X		Lots of surprises
9.	Lots of travel			X			No travel
10.	Closely managed				X		Managed from afar
11.	Work with same group			X			Work with different people
12.	Work indoors			X			Work outside
13.	Highly technical	X					Not technical
14.	Little innovation			X —	—X		Considerable innovation
15.	Short work cycles				X		Long work projects
16.	Low financial risk			X			High financial risk
17.	High attention to detail	X					Low attention to detail
18.	High specialisation		X				Low specialisation
19.	High visibility			X			Low visibility
20.	Extended working hours		X				9–5 job
21.	Many deadlines		X				Few deadlines
22.	Others depend on you		X				Little dependence
23.	Highly structured				X		Little structure
		HD	D	=	D	HD	

Engineering

There is tremendous scope for careers in modern engineering, which needs people with a range of talents. Throughout the country there are many vacancies for technologists. Engineering is creative and involves judgement, scientific understanding, risk-taking, working in teams and facing exciting challenges.

Apart from the engineering industry itself, engineers are sought for many other areas including design, development, quality assurance, industrial engineering patents, consultancy, the oil industry, teaching, and so on. The Civil Service (see page 52) recruits 1000 engineers and scientists annually and all public utilities have recruiting programmes.

According to the Engineering Council there is no age limit for readers considering a career change. Minimum educational standards stated by the Council are:

BTEC National for Engineering Technician
HNC for Incorporated Engineer
Honours degree for Chartered Engineer

The Engineering Council lists 46 different institutes/associations related to the engineering industry. Write to: The Engineering Council, 10 Maltravers Street, London WC2R 3ER for Board for Engineers Registration booklet (enclose sae).

Questionnaire: Civil Engineering

1. Name and address of organisation

   Institution of Civil Engineers,
   1–7 Great George Street, London SW1P 3AA

2. Telephone no

   071-222 7722

3. Fax no

   071-222 7500

4. Typically, for what job(s) does membership of your organisation qualify a person?

   For chartered civil engineer, incorporated engineer and engineering technician posts with contractors, consultants, local government and statutory bodies

5. Up to what age is it practical for our readers to consider a career change to these occupations?

   50–55

6. Minimum education standards necessary

   Chartered civil engineering – A levels plus degree; incorporated engineer HNC/HND; engineering technician ONC

7. Qualifying examinations

   The Institution's professional review

8. Essential experience

   Up to four years' practical work in the industry

9. Desirable experience

   Good, responsible management

10. Training available (course(s) and examples of existing providers)

    (a) Full-time

    At universities, polytechnics and colleges

    (b) Part-time

    At polytechnics and colleges

    (c) Correspondence course

    (d) Distance learning

    Can be set up by special arrangement

    (e) Other

    Continuing education and training is mandatory

11. Additional comments (government grants and other initiatives for mature students, bursaries, etc)

    The ICE Quest Scholarship Scheme is available to assist in supplementing local authority grants. Contact the Civil Engineering Careers Service at the above address for information on career opportunities in civil and structural engineering

Job dimensions: Civil Engineer

Key: HD – Highly Descriptive,   D – Descriptive,   = In the middle

		HD	D	=	D	HD	
1.	Supervise many		X				No supervision
2.	Teamwork	X					Work independently
3.	Customer contact	X					No customer contact
4.	Work in large organisation		X	X			Work alone
5.	Produce goods			X			Provide a service
6.	Fixed salary	X					Paid by results
7.	Flexitime		X				Fixed hours
8.	Routine work		X	X			Lots of surprises
9.	Lots of travel		X	X			No travel
10.	Closely managed			X	X		Managed from afar
11.	Work with same group		X				Work with different people
12.	Work indoors	X				X	Work outside
13.	Highly technical	X					Not technical
14.	Little innovation		X	X			Considerable innovation
15.	Short work cycles			X	X		Long work projects
16.	Low financial risk		X				High financial risk
17.	High attention to detail	X					Low attention to detail
18.	High specialisation		X				Low specialisation
19.	High visibility	X					Low visibility
20.	Extended working hours		X	X			9–5 job
21.	Many deadlines		X				Few deadlines
22.	Others depend on you	X					Little dependence
23.	Highly structured		X				Little structure
		HD	D	=	D	HD	

Questionnaire: Estate Agency

1. Name and address of organisation

   National Association of Estate Agents (NAEA), Arbon House, 21 Jury Street, Warwick CV34 4EH

2. Telephone no

   0926 496800

3. Fax no

   0926 400953

4. Typically, for what job(s) does membership of your organisation qualify a person?

   Estate agency

5. Up to what age is it practical for our readers to consider a career change to these occupations?

   No limit

6. Minimum education standards necessary

7. Qualifying examinations

   None required

8. Essential experience

9. Desirable experience

   Estate agency is essentially a 'people business'. Any experience in dealing with people is therefore helpful

10. Training available (course(s) and examples of existing providers)

    (a) Full-time

    —

    (b) Part-time

    —

    (c) Correspondence course

    NAEA correspondence course. See point 11

    (d) Distance learning

    Certificate in Residential Estate Agency Course. Contact College of Estate Management on 0734 861101

    (e) Other

    The Association organises a wide range of one-day courses

11. Additional comments (government grants and other initiatives for mature students, bursaries, etc)

    The NAEA and the Rapid Results College have produced a home study course for junior negotiators. Contact the RRC, Tuition House, London SW19 4DS or ring 081-947 2211

101

Job dimensions: Estate Agent

Key: HD – Highly Descriptive,   D – Descriptive,   = In the middle

		HD	D	=	D	HD	
1.	Supervise many				X		No supervision
2.	Teamwork	X					Work independently
3.	Customer contact	X					No customer contact
4.	Work in large organisation			X			Work alone
5.	Produce goods				X		Provide a service
6.	Fixed salary				X		Paid by results
7.	Flexitime		X				Fixed hours
8.	Routine work			X			Lots of surprises
9.	Lots of travel			X			No travel
10.	Closely managed			X			Managed from afar
11.	Work with same group				X		Work with different people
12.	Work indoors		X				Work outside
13.	Highly technical			X			Not technical
14.	Little innovation			X			Considerable innovation
15.	Short work cycles	X					Long work projects
16.	Low financial risk		X				High financial risk
17.	High attention to detail	X					Low attention to detail
18.	High specialisation			X			Low specialisation
19.	High visibility	X					Low visibility
20.	Extended working hours		X—	—X			9–5 job
21.	Many deadlines				X		Few deadlines
22.	Others depend on you		X				Little dependence
23.	Highly structured				X		Little structure
		HD	D	=	D	HD	

Housing

Housing in Britain is undergoing substantial change. There are more home owners than ever before; the public sector is having to fight for diminishing resources, fewer new homes are being built, and homelessness is a growing problem.

If you choose to work in housing, you are opting for challenging, often difficult work. But it is also worthwhile and the sense of achievement can be high. Your decisions will affect the quality of people's lives.

If you are considering a career switch, you must first decide whether you have the commitment and talent to enter such an area. In addition, you will need training to give you the requisite knowledge. You will have to work on your own initiative, take difficult decisions and have excellent interpersonal skills. Housing-related work varies considerably from one job to another but there is one common feature: an interest in, and concern for, how and where people live.

The Institute of Housing is the professional body for people working in housing. It is able to offer individual advice across the whole spectrum of housing subjects, including career moves.

There are several different routes to a housing career depending on whether you wish to study full or part time and whether you want to specialise in any particular area of housing.

There are full-time housing degree and diploma courses, and full- and part-time recognised courses as well as the Institute's own degree-level Professional Qualification (PQ) which is studied part time over three/four years. To do the PQ or another part-time recognised course, you will need to have a job in housing already.

There is also a two-year BTEC Higher National Certificate and a range of one-year certified part-time courses for specialist jobs, such as wardens or repairs and maintenance staff.

Housing jobs are found predominantly with local councils and housing associations, but trusts, voluntary bodies and the private sector provide others.

Check the national and local press and find out whether your local council publishes a list of job vacancies. Most jobs are advertised in *Inside Housing* (published weekly by Inside Communications, Octavia House, Westwood Business Park, Westwood Way, Coventry CV4 8JP and *Housing Associations Weekly* (published by the National Federation of Housing Associations, 175 Gray's Inn Road, London WC1X 8UP).

If you would like to know more about a career in housing contact the Institute of Housing, Octavia House, Westwood Business Park, Westwood Way, Coventry CV4 8JP; 0203 694433; Fax 0203 695110.

Job dimensions: Housing Manager

Key: HD – Highly Descriptive, D – Descriptive, = In the middle

		HD	D	=	D	HD	
1.	Supervise many		X				No supervision
2.	Teamwork	X					Work independently
3.	Customer contact	X					No customer contact
4.	Work in large organisation		X				Work alone
5.	Produce goods					X	Provide a service
6.	Fixed salary	X					Paid by results
7.	Flexitime					X	Fixed hours
8.	Routine work		X—	—X			Lots of surprises
9.	Lots of travel				X		No travel
10.	Closely managed				X		Managed from afar
11.	Work with same group		X				Work with different people
12.	Work indoors		X—	—X			Work outside
13.	Highly technical		X				Not technical
14.	Little innovation			X			Considerable innovation
15.	Short work cycles	X—			—X		Long work projects
16.	Low financial risk	X					High financial risk
17.	High attention to detail	X					Low attention to detail
18.	High specialisation		X				Low specialisation
19.	High visibility	X					Low visibility
20.	Extended working hours					X	9–5 job
21.	Many deadlines				X		Few deadlines
22.	Others depend on you		X				Little dependence
23.	Highly structured		X				Little structure
		HD	D	=	D	HD	

105

Questionnaire: Landscape Architecture

1. Name and address of organisation

   The Landscape Institute,
   6–7 Barnard Mews, London SW11 1QU

2. Telephone no

   071-738 9166

3. Typically, for what job(s) does membership of your organisation qualify a person?

   A career as a landscape architect, landscape scientist or landscape manager

4. Up to what age is it practical for our readers to consider a career change to these occupations?

   No age limit but those considering a change need to be aware that it takes seven years to qualify as a landscape architect if starting from undergraduate level. However, it is possible to study part-time while working

5. Minimum education standards necessary

   Usually two A levels in relevant subjects or landscape management

6. Qualifying examinations

   Accredited landscape architecture course or a course relevant to landscape management or science followed by the professional practice examination

7. Essential experience

   Two years' practical experience prior to taking the professional practice examination. Landscape managers and landscape scientists must have relevant work experience before becoming graduate members

8. Training available (course(s) and examples of existing providers)

   (a) Full-time

   Three years full-time, one year in practice and one-year full-time courses for undergraduates; two-year course for graduates

   (b) Part-time

   Four to five years for undergraduates; three to four years for graduates

   (c) Other

   Courses judged by the Institute to be relevant to landscape management or landscape science

11. Additional comments (government grants and other initiatives for mature students, bursaries, etc)

    The Institute can supply a list of colleges conducting appropriate courses

Job dimensions: Landscape Architect

Key: HD – Highly Descriptive,   D – Descriptive,   = In the middle

		HD	D	=	D	HD	
1.	Supervise many		X				No supervision
2.	Teamwork	X					Work independently
3.	Customer contact		X				No customer contact
4.	Work in large organisation		X	X			Work alone
5.	Produce goods				X		Provide a service
6.	Fixed salary	X					Paid by results
7.	Flexitime				X		Fixed hours
8.	Routine work		X				Lots of surprises
9.	Lots of travel		X				No travel
10.	Closely managed				X		Managed from afar
11.	Work with same group		X				Work with different people
12.	Work indoors		X	X			Work outside
13.	Highly technical	X					Not technical
14.	Little innovation			X			Considerable innovation
15.	Short work cycles			X	X		Long work projects
16.	Low financial risk	X	X				High financial risk
17.	High attention to detail	X					Low attention to detail
18.	High specialisation	X					Low specialisation
19.	High visibility	X					Low visibility
20.	Extended working hours			X	X		9–5 job
21.	Many deadlines		X				Few deadlines
22.	Others depend on you		X				Little dependence
23.	Highly structured		X	X			Little structure
		HD	D	=	D	HD	

Questionnaire: Motor Industry

1. Name and address of organisation

   The Institute of the Motor Industry, Fanshaws, Brickendon, Hertford SG13 8PG

2. Telephone no

   0992 86521

3. Fax no

   0992 86548

4. Typically, for what job(s) does membership of your organisation qualify a person?

   All jobs within the motor industry

5. Up to what age is it practical for our readers to consider a career change to these occupations?

   No age limit

6. Minimum education standards necessary

   Four GCSEs – maths and English, plus two others

7. Qualifying examinations

   Certificate of Manager; Higher Certificate of Manager, Diploma and Degree

8. Essential experience

   All members of this Institute need experience

9. Desirable experience

   —

10. Training available (course(s) and examples of existing providers)

    (a) Full-time

    There are full-time motor vehicle courses at various colleges throughout the country

    (b) Part-time

    As above

    (c) Correspondence course

    —

    (d) Distance learning

    Open learning Certificate of Management

    (e) Other

    The Institute is developing courses for all jobs within the industry

11. Additional comments (government grants and other initiatives for mature students, bursaries, etc)

    There are grants available from companies within the motor industry

Job dimensions: Manager, Motor Industry

Key: HD – Highly Descriptive, D – Descriptive, = In the middle

		HD	D	=	D	HD	
1.	Supervise many		X				No supervision
2.	Teamwork	X					Work independently
3.	Customer contact	X					No customer contact
4.	Work in large organisation	X		X			Work alone
5.	Produce goods			X			Provide a service
6.	Fixed salary		X		X		Paid by results
7.	Flexitime				X	X	Fixed hours
8.	Routine work		X				Lots of surprises
9.	Lots of travel				X		No travel
10.	Closely managed			X			Managed from afar
11.	Work with same group	X					Work with different people
12.	Work indoors	X		X			Work outside
13.	Highly technical			X			Not technical
14.	Little innovation		X				Considerable innovation
15.	Short work cycles	X					Long work projects
16.	Low financial risk	X					High financial risk
17.	High attention to detail			X	X		Low attention to detail
18.	High specialisation				X		Low specialisation
19.	High visibility	X					Low visibility
20.	Extended working hours			X			9–5 job
21.	Many deadlines	X					Few deadlines
22.	Others depend on you	X					Little dependence
23.	Highly structured	X					Little structure
		HD	D	=	D	HD	

Plumbing

Plumbing is one of the courses available under Employment Training. A typical course leads to the City and Guilds of London Craft Certificate in Plumbing. The theoretical content over one year allows the trainee to complete the first of two years of Craft Certificate studies. Such a course is based on one day a week on theory and in the workshop at the college and four days a week at work placement.

The Institute of Plumbing is a professional society, registered as an educational charity. Its main objective is to develop the science and practice of plumbing. The Institute maintains the Register of Plumbers initiated by the Worshipful Company of Plumbers in July 1886 to identify competent and responsible plumbers.

Questionnaire: Plumbing

1. Name and address of organisation

   The Institute of Plumbing, 64 Station Lane, Hornchurch, Essex RM12 6NB

2. Telephone no

   0708 472791

3. Fax no

   0708 451199

4. Typically, for what job(s) does membership of your organisation qualify a person?

   Plumber, consultant/designer, lecturer

5. Up to what age is it practical for our readers to consider a career change to these occupations?

   Approximately 40

6. Minimum education standards necessary

   City and Guilds

7. Qualifying examinations

   —

8. Essential experience

9. Desirable experience

   } Five years

10. Training available (course(s) and examples of existing providers)

    (a) Full-time

    (b) Part-time

    } City and Guilds – Employment Training. See page 171

    (c) Correspondence course

    —

    (d) Distance learning

    —

    (e) Other

    Seminars

11. Additional comments (government grants and other initiatives for mature students, bursaries, etc)

    —

Job dimensions: Plumber

Key: HD – Highly Descriptive, D – Descriptive, = In the middle

	HD	D	=	D	HD	
1. Supervise many				X		No supervision
2. Teamwork				X		Work independently
3. Customer contact	X		ᵃ			No customer contact
4. Work in large organisation			X——X			Work alone
5. Produce goods				X		Provide a service
6. Fixed salary			X——X			Paid by results
7. Flexitime	X					Fixed hours
8. Routine work	X					Lots of surprises
9. Lots of travel		X——X				No travel
10. Closely managed			X——X		X	Managed from afar
11. Work with same group				X		Work with different people
12. Work indoors		X				Work outside
13. Highly technical			X			Not technical
14. Little innovation		X				Considerable innovation
15. Short work cycles	X					Long work projects
16. Low financial risk	X					High financial risk
17. High attention to detail			X			Low attention to detail
18. High specialisation				X		Low specialisation
19. High visibility	X					Low visibility
20. Extended working hours		X				9–5 job
21. Many deadlines		X				Few deadlines
22. Others depend on you	X					Little dependence
23. Highly structured				X		Little structure
	HD	D	=	D	HD	

Questionnaire: Surveying

1. Name and address of organisation

Royal Institution of Chartered Surveyors (RICS), 12 Great George Street, London SW1P 3AD

2. Telephone no

071-222 7000 Ext 228

3. Fax no

071-222 9430

4. Typically, for what job(s) does membership of your organisation qualify a person?

All seven surveying divisions: general practice (including estate agency, commercial property, chattels, plant and machinery, etc); quantity surveying; building surveying; rural practice; land and hydrographic) surveying; minerals (and marine resources); planning/development

5. Up to what age is it practical for our readers to consider a career change to these occupations?

—

6. Minimum education standards necessary

Five passes at GCSE/A level but see points 8 and 9 below

7. Qualifying examinations

Assessment of Professional Competence (APC) consists of two years' practical diary work; simulated work situation (under exact conditions); followed by interview if successful at APC (taken after fully exempting degree or equivalent)

8. Training available (course(s) and examples of existing providers)

Write to the Institution for its comprehensive careers brochure which gives details regarding education standards and the various courses available. These include full-time or sandwich courses. While employed in a surveyor's office, you can study on a part-time, day release or distance-taught course

9. Additional comments (government grants and other initiatives for mature students, bursaries, etc)

RICS operates a Direct Membership Entry for those over 35 with 15 years' approved experience (ie irrespective of academic qualifications)

Job dimensions: Chartered Surveyor

Key: HD – Highly Descriptive,   D – Descriptive,   = In the middle

		HD	D	=	D	HD	
1.	Supervise many		X				No supervision
2.	Teamwork	X	X				Work independently
3.	Customer contact		X		X		No customer contact
4.	Work in large organisation				X	X	Work alone
5.	Produce goods				X		Provide a service
6.	Fixed salary	X					Paid by results
7.	Flexitime					X	Fixed hours
8.	Routine work		X				Lots of surprises
9.	Lots of travel		X		X		No travel
10.	Closely managed					X	Managed from afar
11.	Work with same group		X		X		Work with different people
12.	Work indoors	X				X	Work outside
13.	Highly technical	X					Not technical
14.	Little innovation		X				Considerable innovation
15.	Short work cycles		X		X		Long work projects
16.	Low financial risk			X			High financial risk
17.	High attention to detail	X					Low attention to detail
18.	High specialisation		X		X		Low specialisation
19.	High visibility				X		Low visibility
20.	Extended working hours				X		9–5 job
21.	Many deadlines		X		X		Few deadlines
22.	Others depend on you	X					Little dependence
23.	Highly structured					X	Little structure
		HD	D	=	D	HD	

Town Planning

There are over 500 government, local authority and development corporation offices in which planners are employed. Increasing numbers of planners work in the private sector, including development, industry and in over 1000 consultancies. Town and country planning is a broad subject and is influenced by many different pressures – political, social and economic. Planning work is varied. All parts of the country face different problems. In small planning offices you will handle a wide range of work, while in a large office you are more likely to be able to specialise. Planners need to make sound judgements, and co-ordination of the necessary information can include basic survey work, research, analysis of data and presentation of possible options and their likely effects. Look at the questionnaire on page 116 and write for the booklets if the scope of the work interests you. Mature students in particular may be interested in the recently developed Joint Distance Learning Diploma. Having studied the booklets, make an appointment to see a planning officer in your local authority for an informal chat.

Questionnaire: Town Planning

1. Name and address of organisation

   The Royal Town Planning Institute (RTPI), 26 Portland Place, London W1N 4BE

2. Telephone no

   071-636 9107

3. Fax no

   071-323 1582

4. Typically, for what job(s) does membership of your organisation qualify a person?

   Practising as a town planner in local or central government, consultancy, architectural practices, development, in other agencies, eg water authorities, British Rail and the private sector

5. Up to what age is it practical for our readers to consider a career change to these occupations?

   No bar – practicalities may influence prospective trainees, eg taking a drop in salary as a trainee. But planning is frequently a postgraduate qualification

6. Minimum education standards necessary

   Those specified by the polytechnic/university running course. Mature entrants generally encouraged

7. Qualifying examinations

   A degree or diploma accredited by the RTPI

8. Essential experience

   For RTPI membership two years' relevant planning experience plus academic qualification

9. Desirable experience

   Variable according to employer – could be from a wide variety of backgrounds, eg architecture, surveying, ecology, etc

10. Training available (course(s) and examples of existing providers)

    (a) Full-time

    (b) Part-time

    (c) Correspondence course

    (d) Distance learning

    (e) Other

    Undergraduate and postgraduate. See point 11

11. Additional comments (government grants and other initiatives for mature students, bursaries, etc)

    Write to the Institute for their booklet 'Careers in Town Planning' and the general information about membership which lists accredited courses

Job dimensions: Town Planner

Key: HD – Highly Descriptive, D – Descriptive, = In the middle

		HD	D	=	D	HD	
1.	Supervise many		X				No supervision
2.	Teamwork	X					Work independently
3.	Customer contact		X		X		No customer contact
4.	Work in large organisation		X		X		Work alone
5.	Produce goods				X		Provide a service
6.	Fixed salary	X					Paid by results
7.	Flexitime		X		X		Fixed hours
8.	Routine work		X				Lots of surprises
9.	Lots of travel			X			No travel
10.	Closely managed		X				Managed from afar
11.	Work with same group		X				Work with different people
12.	Work indoors		X	X			Work outside
13.	Highly technical		X				Not technical
14.	Little innovation		X				Considerable innovation
15.	Short work cycles	X				X	Long work projects
16.	Low financial risk	X					High financial risk
17.	High attention to detail	X					Low attention to detail
18.	High specialisation		X				Low specialisation
19.	High visibility			X			Low visibility
20.	Extended working hours		X			X	9–5 job
21.	Many deadlines		X				Few deadlines
22.	Others depend on you		X				Little dependence
23.	Highly structured		X				Little structure
		HD	D	=	D	HD	

C. Hotel, Leisure and Retail Industries

Hotel, Catering and Institutional Management

The hospitality industry is Britain's second largest employer and makes a major contribution to the economy and social well-being of the country. As a service industry, it has to be highly responsive to the changing business, social and leisure needs of people wanting food, drink and accommodation away from home, and for all the personal service that goes with these needs. Hotels and catering services are often international operations; not only do multinational companies operate in the UK but many companies have developed extensive hotel and leisure operations throughout the world, to say nothing of 'hotel services' in hospitals, at construction sites, and so on, worldwide. However, there are also many small businesses with a limited number of staff who work closely together as a team.

This industry offers worthwhile and challenging careers at all levels, especially in management, with great opportunities for responsibility and advancement, often at an early age. It offers both the demands and the satisfactions involved in providing a caring service for people of all nations and in every walk of life, both at home and abroad. The scope of the industry is not always appreciated. For example, it offers careers in: hotels, guest houses and restaurants of all kinds; pubs, clubs, inns, steak bars and cafés; motels and motorway catering services; holiday centres and tourist attractions; civic catering and leisure complexes; staff restaurants and works canteens; school and college catering. It also involves domestic service in homes and special schools, as well as in colleges and universities; 'hotel' services in hospitals; catering for the Armed Forces; airways, marine and rail catering.

A professionally based training scheme for hotel and catering workers is included in Employment Training (ET). See page 171.

Questionnaire: Hotel Catering

1. Name and address of organisation

   Hotel Catering and Institutional Management Association (HCIMA), 191 Trinity Road, London SW17 7HN

2. Telephone no

   081-672 4251

3. Fax no

   081-682 1707

4. Typically, for what job(s) does membership of your organisation qualify a person?

   Completion of our professional diploma (our higher level programme) fits the student for a career in hotel and catering management. Completion of the certificate is preparation for a career at supervisory level. Full membership of the HCIMA reflects a member's higher level education and management experience in our industry

5. Up to what age is it practical for our readers to consider a career change to these occupations?

   Within this industry there is no clear age limit. The individuals' personality and presentation are their skill

6. Minimum education standards necessary

   The standard of education required will clearly be reflected in the level of responsibility achieved by each individual. A good understanding of the English language and maths is essential for jobs such as waiter/waitress, bar staff or reception

7. Qualifications

   Hotel and Catering is among the first industries in the UK to introduce the government's new National Vocational Qualification. From January 1992 NVQs are replacing traditional craft and supervisory qualifications. Degrees will remain as before for the time being. To qualify for full corporate membership of the Association, the individual must hold an HND/degree or our diploma programme supported by at least three years' managerial experience

10. Training available

    (a) Full-time

    City & Guilds Colleges will continue to offer full-time courses at craft and operative level. These are likely to be linked to NVQs at levels 1 and 2

    BTEC – National Diploma in Hotel and Catering Operations. HND in Hotel, Catering and Institutional Management

    Students may gain NVQ units during completion of the above studies

    SCOTVEC – National Certificate, etc

    HND in Hotel, Catering and Institutional Management

119

Students will gain nine SVQ units as a result of completing these qualifications

Degree courses in hotel and catering subjects.

Post-graduate diplomas and certificates

(b) Part-time including flexible/distance study modes

All those working in the industry and involved in part-time training or on industry-based training schemes will work towards NVQs

NVQ level 1 = basic skills
NVQ level 2 = craft and operative competences
NVQ level 3 = supervisory competences
NVQ level 4 = first line management competences

College courses will be designed to provide learning support for NVQs

The HCIMA Professional Certificate provides learning support for NVQs level 3

The HCIMA Professional Diploma provides learning support for NVQs level 4

11. Additional comments (government grants and other initiatives for mature students, bursaries, etc)

HCIMA produces information sheets which detail the opportunities, the grades of membership, colleges which offer suitable courses and grant possibilities

Job dimensions: Hotel Manager

Key: HD – Highly Descriptive, D – Descriptive, = In the middle

		HD	D	=	D	HD	
1.	Supervise many	X					No supervision
2.	Teamwork	X					Work independently
3.	Customer contact	X					No customer contact
4.	Work in large organisation		X—X				Work alone
5.	Produce goods			X—X			Provide a service
6.	Fixed salary		X				Paid by results
7.	Flexitime			X			Fixed hours
8.	Routine work			X			Lots of surprises
9.	Lots of travel				X		No travel
10.	Closely managed		X———X				Managed from afar
11.	Work with same group		X				Work with different people
12.	Work indoors	X					Work outside
13.	Highly technical				X		Not technical
14.	Little innovation			X			Considerable innovation
15.	Short work cycles	X					Long work projects
16.	Low financial risk			X			High financial risk
17.	High attention to detail			X			Low attention to detail
18.	High specialisation			X			Low specialisation
19.	High visibility	X					Low visibility
20.	Extended working hours	X					9–5 job
21.	Many deadlines		X				Few deadlines
22.	Others depend on you	X					Little dependence
23.	Highly structured		X———X				Little structure
		HD	D	=	D	HD	

The Leisure Industry

The leisure industry is a term for a range of organisations which cater for people's leisure interests including sports, entertainments, parks and outdoor activities, theatre, cultural pursuits, tourist attractions and the arts. The leisure industry is growing and the amount of money people spend on leisure is increasing – and so is the number of people employed in the industry in a wide range of jobs.

There are three main groupings within the leisure industry:

- The public sector. Local authorities and public bodies are major providers of sports and leisure centres, parks, pools, theatres, community centres, sports grounds, tourist information centres, and so on.
- The private sector. Commercial interests control a substantial proportion of the industry, with investments in cinemas, theatres, hotels, pubs, theme parks, discos, health clubs and the like.
- The voluntary sector. There are many opportunities to gain experience by offering your services on a voluntary basis to local clubs and societies, conservation groups, arts centres and play schemes.

Unlike many industries, leisure is a fairly 'open' industry in terms of promotion prospects. Although an increasing number of people enter the industry with higher education qualifications, it is certainly possible for entrants with related experience to work their way up from a lower position to management level. The diagram opposite indicates the range of responsibilities in the industry, and the questionnaire is on page 124.

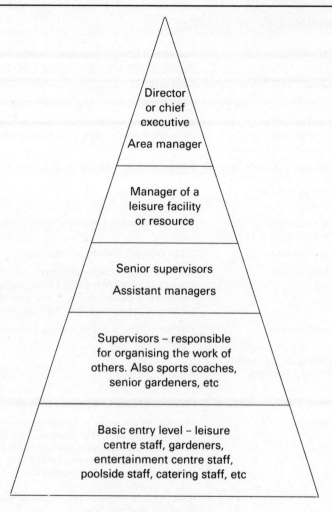

The leisure industry

Questionnaire: Leisure Industry

1. Name and address of organisation

Institute of Leisure and Amenity Management (ILAM), Lower Basildon, Reading, Berks RG8 9NE

2. Telephone no

0491 874222

3. Fax no

0491 874059

4. Typically, for what job(s) does membership of your organisation qualify a person?

Management posts in the leisure industry – although ILAM is not a 'qualifying association' in the traditional sense

5. Up to what age is it practical for our readers to consider a career change to these occupations?

Certainly up to mid-40s; maybe beyond

6. Minimum education standards necessary

To enter industry – motivation and common sense!

7. Qualifying examinations

ILAM Certificate and ILAM Diploma

8. Essential experience

For Certificate membership three years' experience in a leisure environment; for Diploma membership five years' experience. The ILAM qualification scheme is being revised in the light of N/SVQs

9. Desirable experience

For management posts, business or supervisory experience

10. Training available (course(s) and examples of existing providers)

   (a) Full-time

HND/Certificate and Degree courses

   (b) Part-time

Many different types of college conduct modular part-time courses; BTEC Continuing Education Certificate (Leisure Management) and SCOTVEC HNC Leisure Managment courses give substantial exemption from ILAM Certificate

   (c) Distance learning

   (d) Other

A distance learning CECert (Leisure Management) course is now available.

11. Additional comments (government grants and other initiatives for mature students, bursaries, etc)

Write for the leaflets 'Guide to Courses in Leisure Management' and 'Careers in the Leisure Industry'

Job dimensions: Manager, Leisure Facility

Key: HD – Highly Descriptive,   D – Descriptive,   = In the middle

		HD	D	=	D	HD	
1.	Supervise many	X					No supervision
2.	Teamwork	X					Work independently
3.	Customer contact	X					No customer contact
4.	Work in large organisation	X					Work alone
5.	Produce goods			X		X	Provide a service
6.	Fixed salary		X		X		Paid by results
7.	Flexitime			X			Fixed hours
8.	Routine work			X			Lots of surprises
9.	Lots of travel				X		No travel
10.	Closely managed			X			Managed from afar
11.	Work with same group		X				Work with different people
12.	Work indoors	X				X	Work outside
13.	Highly technical			X			Not technical
14.	Little innovation		X				Considerable innovation
15.	Short work cycles		X				Long work projects
16.	Low financial risk		X				High financial risk
17.	High attention to detail	X					Low attention to detail
18.	High specialisation			X			Low specialisation
19.	High visibility	X					Low visibility
20.	Extended working hours		X		X		9–5 job
21.	Many deadlines				X		Few deadlines
22.	Others depend on you	X					Little dependence
23.	Highly structured		X				Little structure
		HD	D	=	D	HD	

125

The Retail Industry

The retail industry has many attractions for people who wish to find employment near their home. One-tenth of the working population is engaged in retail and distribution. The industry is changing rapidly with the growth of large shopping precincts outside major towns. Inevitably, a major supermarket takes a prime position in such developments.

Women with children of school age will appreciate the opportunities which the multiple retailers offer for work on a full-time or part-time basis. One national supermarket offers full training, subsidised restaurants with three-course lunches for 44p and full breakfast for 16p, a pension scheme for part-time and full-time staff, free life assurance, and a uniform. After a probationary period, staff enjoy at least four weeks' paid leave entitlement, 10 per cent discount on staff purchases and participation in a profit-sharing scheme. There is generous maternity/paternity leave. Salaries are competitive, with a premium rate payable for Saturday work. A spell of temporary work, to give you the taste of the retail industry, will provide an opportunity to consider whether you want to train for a managerial post.

Boots the Chemists

For more than a century Boots has been a familiar name on the high street. More than 1000 stores throughout the UK, a product range exceeding 50,000 items and a group turnover of £2500 million bear testimony to the size of the company.

Boots has kept pace with the many changes in today's modern retailing but has never lost sight of the fact that its staff are its greatest asset. Boots looks for energy and genuine enthusiasm in people wishing to make the most of a career in modern retailing. It also realises that some people have different needs, and that is why its attitude is as flexible as possible. In Boots the Chemists you can work full time, part time or on a flexible contract, which will allow you to work a set number of hours a week on an arrangement that suits you. You won't need to work school holidays, but because you'll be a permanent employee you'll share in all the usual company benefits. If you take up a supervisory role in a store, you can also take advantage of the job-share scheme. The Boots Career Break, on the other hand, offers a break from employment for up to five years.

Boots also has a rapidly expanding opticians' chain, and the Children's World superstores provide a unique environment for family shopping. A further option for growth has come through the acquisition of Halfords, Payless and A G Stanley.

Boots is also a major industrial group and exports to over 140 countries.

Whatever kind of position or contract you're interested in, you'll benefit from a thorough training, career opportunities and a friendly atmosphere.

If you would like to find out more information about opportunities in Boots the Chemists, please contact the personnel officer or the manager at your local store.

Job dimensions: Manager, Retail Industry

Key: HD – Highly Descriptive, D – Descriptive, = In the middle

		HD	D	=	D	HD	
1.	Supervise many	X					No supervision
2.	Teamwork	X					Work independently
3.	Customer contact	X					No customer contact
4.	Work in large organisation		X—X				Work alone
5.	Produce goods					X	Provide a service
6.	Fixed salary	X					Paid by results
7.	Flexitime	X——X					Fixed hours
8.	Routine work		X				Lots of surprises
9.	Lots of travel					X	No travel
10.	Closely managed	X					Managed from afar
11.	Work with same group	X					Work with different people
12.	Work indoors	X					Work outside
13.	Highly technical			X			Not technical
14.	Little innovation				X		Considerable innovation
15.	Short work cycles		X				Long work projects
16.	Low financial risk	X					High financial risk
17.	High attention to detail		X				Low attention to detail
18.	High specialisation			X			Low specialisation
19.	High visibility	X					Low visibility
20.	Extended working hours			X			9–5 job
21.	Many deadlines	X					Few deadlines
22.	Others depend on you	X					Little dependence
23.	Highly structured	X					Little structure
		HD	D	=	D	HD	

Questionnaire: Travel Agency

1. Name and address of organisation — Association of British Travel Agents, National Training Board, 11–17 Chertsey Road, Woking, Surrey GU21 5AL

2. Telephone no — 0483 727321

3. Fax no — 0483 756698

4. Typically, for what job(s) does membership of your organisation qualify a person? — Positions with travel agents and tour operators

5. Up to what age is it practical for our readers to consider a career change to these occupations? — 40–45

6. Minimum education standards necessary — No formal academic requirements necessary for entry at base level

7. Qualifying examinations — —

8. Essential experience — —

9. Desirable experience — Previous experience in dealing with the general public

10. Training available (course(s) and examples of existing providers)

    (a) Full-time — Certificate in Travel Studies (ABTA/CGLI 499) one year

    (b) Part-time — Certificate of Travel Agency Competence (COTAC) Level I. Certificate of Tour Operating Practice (COTOP) Level I

    (c) Correspondence course — —

    (d) Distance learning — Preparation for COTAC and COTOP can both be undertaken on a self-study basis via the ABTA NTB college of open learning

    (e) Other — —

11. Additional comments (government grants and other initiatives for mature students, bursaries, etc) — ABTA Employment Training (ET) scheme

129

Job dimensions: Travel Agent

Key: HD – Highly Descriptive,   D – Descriptive,   = In the middle

		HD	D	=	D	HD	
1.	Supervise many		X				No supervision
2.	Teamwork	X					Work independently
3.	Customer contact	X					No customer contact
4.	Work in large organisation		X—	X			Work alone
5.	Produce goods				X		Provide a service
6.	Fixed salary			X———		X	Paid by results
7.	Flexitime		X———	X			Fixed hours
8.	Routine work		X———	X			Lots of surprises
9.	Lots of travel	X ——	X				No travel
10.	Closely managed			X			Managed from afar
11.	Work with same group	X					Work with different people
12.	Work indoors	X					Work outside
13.	Highly technical		X				Not technical
14.	Little innovation		X—	—X			Considerable innovation
15.	Short work cycles	X					Long work projects
16.	Low financial risk		X				High financial risk
17.	High attention to detail	X					Low attention to detail
18.	High specialisation		X—	X			Low specialisation
19.	High visibility	X					Low visibility
20.	Extended working hours		X ——	—X			9–5 job
21.	Many deadlines		X				Few deadlines
22.	Others depend on you	X					Little dependence
23.	Highly structured		X				Little structure
		HD	D	=	D	HD	

D. Professional Services

Accountancy

We forecast that accountants will continue to be in increasing demand in the 1990s. Those who qualify can choose to specialise in various ways – in taxation, audit, consultancy and work for professional accountancy practices or public organisations. (Accountants are mentioned in the sections on the Civil Service and local authorities, pages 55 and 66) Many company directors have used an accounting qualification as the basis for a successful career.

The work of the Chartered Institute of Public Finance and Accountancy is described below. It is followed by detailed questionnaires completed by the Institute of Chartered Accountants in England and Wales and the Chartered Association of Certified Accountants.

The Chartered Institute of Public Finance and Accountancy (CIPFA)

Each accountancy qualification has its own particular emphasis. CIPFA trains financial managers who specialise in the skills required for the challenges of public finance and accountancy.

CIPFA members hold positions of responsibility in over 1500 organisations, including local authorities, central government, the National Health Service and National Audit, as well as in major accountancy firms, building societies and other parts of the private sector.

CIPFA membership appeals particularly to those interested in the effective management of public services for the common good. Although the boundaries between the private and public sectors are becoming less clear-cut, a basic concern common to both – the efficient financial management of limited resources – remains the same. Managers in public service organisations must also take into account non-financial indicators of performance. Some of these – for example, the quality of different forms of patient care in the health service – can be difficult to measure. The financial manager must respond sensitively to the complex challenges which may result from the need to consider more than just the financial aspects.

CIPFA's three-year education and training scheme is designed to develop practical skills in addition to teaching the theoretical basis of accountancy. The syllabus reflects the increasing commercial emphasis in the public sector and management is a core element. Structured on-the-job training is a requirement of the scheme, as are block- or day-release courses at an approved local college during office hours. The scheme is run by the Institute in conjunction with approved employers to ensure that the standard of training remains high, thus maintaining a low drop-out rate and high pass rates.

A CIPFA qualification offers job variety, job mobility, job security and excellent career prospects.

CIPFA recruits students from A level, the Association of Accounting Technicians, and graduate levels and has a considerable number of mature students in their 30s and 40s. To be accepted as a CIPFA student, you must first obtain a trainee appointment in a financial capacity with an approved employer. Many advertise in the national and local newspapers. The best source of information on vacancies for graduate trainees is the Institute's Directory of Graduate Opportunities, available from your local career service or CIPFA. For information on CIPFA for students of all backgrounds, obtain a copy of 'The Students' Guide to CIPFA – Professional Education and Training'.

Experienced public service accountants and auditors should obtain the booklet 'The CIPFA Senior Officers' Scheme' which indicates the special arrangements for such students taking the qualification.

Write to the Recruitment Liaison Officer, CIPFA, 3 Robert Street, London WC2N 6BH; 071-895 8823 Ext 262; Fax 071-930 6187.

Questionnaire: Chartered Accountant

1. Name and address of organisation

The Institute of Chartered Accountants in England and Wales, Chartered Accountants' Hall, Moorgate Place, London EC2P 2BJ

2. Telephone no

071-628 7060

3. Fax no

071-920 0547

4. Typically, for what job(s) does membership of your organisation qualify a person?

The ICAEW is one of the world's leading accountancy bodies. Around half the Institute's members work in public practice as sole practitioners, partners or employees in accountancy firms. Chartered accountants also play a major role in industry and commerce, working not only in finance functions but also as general managers and frequently at very senior levels

5. Up to what age is it practical for our readers to consider a career change to these occupations?

There is no upper age limit for entry to training but applicants over 35 have more difficulty in securing a training contract

6. Minimum education standards necessary	Five GCSE/GCE passes, including English language and mathematics, two of which must be at A level (or equivalent, eg BTEC National) followed by the successful completion of a degree in any subject, or a Foundation Course, or the AAT qualification (achieved with credit or distinction in the Final Examination)
7. Qualifying examinations	The Professional Examinations are set by the Institute
8. Essential experience	A three- or four-year training contract with an authorised training office. These offices are primarily firms of chartered accountants although training is now available in a growing number of industrial and commercial organisations
9. Desirable experience	None, although applicants should have the ability to communicate well both orally and in writing and to work as part of a team
10. Training available (course(s) and examples of existing providers)	
(a) Full-time (b) Part-time	The training contract combines work experience and in-house training with study leave, which is usually block release, to prepare for the examinations. Examination tuition is provided by specialist tutorial organisations
(c) Correspondence course (d) Distance learning	Not available
(e) Other	Not applicable
11. Additional comments (government grants and other initiatives for mature students, bursaries, etc)	At the Institute's discretion, applicants over 25 who lack formal educational qualifications but who have obtained a minimum of seven years' 'acceptable' accountancy experience may have entry requirements waived. Those wishing to investigate this option should contact the Student Registration Section at the Institute (ext 3274) A part-time training contract requires a minimum of 21 working hours per week

NB A careers brochure and 'Training Vacancies' which lists many of the firms currently recruiting, are available from the Student Recruitment Section at the Institute or from local careers services. A separate brochure containing information about Training Outside Public Practice (TOPP) and details of TOPP vacancies is also available

Readers in Scotland may write to: The Institute of Chartered Accountants of Scotland, 27 Queen Street, Edinburgh, EH2 1LA, or telephone 031-225 5673

Questionnaire: Certified Accountant

1. Name and address of organisation

   The Chartered Association of Certified Accountants, 29 Lincoln's Inn Fields, London WC2A 3EE

2. Telephone no

   071-242 6855

3. Fax no

   071-831 8054

4. Typically, for what job(s) does membership of your organisation qualify a person?

   Accountant, auditor, financial director, company secretary, managing director

5. Up to what age is it practical for our readers to consider a career change to these occupations?

   55

6. Minimum education standards necessary

   Normally two A levels plus three O levels but see point 11

7. Qualifying examinations

   Levels 1, 2, 3

8. Essential experience

   Minimum of three years in a range of accounting functions

9. Desirable experience

   —

10. Training available (course(s) and examples of existing providers)

    (a) Full-time

    (b) Part-time

    (c) Correspondence course

    } Yes. See point 11

    (d) Distance learning

    ACCA/Open College. See point 11

    (e) Other

    Longman/ACCA manuals

11. Additional comments (government grants and other initiatives for mature students, bursaries, etc)

    Mandatory and discretionary grants available for full-time students. Employers are often willing to employ older students – see various lists. Write to the Association for their leaflet 'How to Become a Certified Accountant' which lists colleges/polytechnics, leaflet on the Open Learning Study programme, and the Longman/ACCA textbook series. This also contains details of the Mature Student Entry Route (MSER)

    NB Employers often sponsor students throughout their training

Job dimensions: Accountant

Key: HD – Highly Descriptive, D – Descriptive, = In the middle

	HD	D	=	D	HD	
1. Supervise many		X		X		No supervision
2. Teamwork		X		X		Work independently
3. Customer contact	X					No customer contact
4. Work in large organisation		X		X		Work alone
5. Produce goods					X	Provide a service
6. Fixed salary	X					Paid by results
7. Flexitime				X		Fixed hours
8. Routine work		X				Lots of surprises
9. Lots of travel		X		X		No travel
10. Closely managed		X				Managed from afar
11. Work with same group		X		X		Work with different people
12. Work indoors	X					Work outside
13. Highly technical		X				Not technical
14. Little innovation			X			Considerable innovation
15. Short work cycles		X		X		Long work projects
16. Low financial risk		X				High financial risk
17. High attention to detail	X					Low attention to detail
18. High specialisation		X				Low specialisation
19. High visibility			X			Low visibility
20. Extended working hours			X			9–5 job
21. Many deadlines	X					Few deadlines
22. Others depend on you	X					Little dependence
23. Highly structured	X					Little structure
	HD	D	=	D	HD	

Questionnaire: Actuarial Work

1. Name and address of organisation

   Institute of Actuaries, Napier House, 4 Worcester Street, Oxford OX1 2AW

2. Telephone no

   0865 794144

3. Fax no

   0865 794094

4. Typically, for what job(s) does membership of your organisation qualify a person?

   Actuarial work in insurance and pensions

5. Up to what age is it practical for our readers to consider a career change to these occupations?

   Up to 40 – although there have been exceptions

6. Minimum education standards necessary

   Grade A or B in mathematics at A level or equivalent

7. Qualifying examinations

   Ten subjects for Fellowship

8. Essential experience

9. Desirable experience

   To qualify as a Fellow you must have three years' acceptable experience

10. Training available (course(s) and examples of existing providers)

    (a) Full-time

    Postgraduate one-year course at City University/ Heriot Watt University

    (b) Part-time

    Postgraduate two-year course at City University

    (c) Correspondence course

    Available for all subjects from the Institute's Education Service

    (d) Distance learning

    —

    (e) Other

    Tutorials, short courses provided by the Institute's Education Service

11. Additional comments (government grants and other initiatives for mature students, bursaries, etc)

    Generally advisable to pass some of the earlier subjects while in current employment before seeking employment as an actuarial trainee. Literature available from the Institute: 'Student Handbook', 'Becoming an Actuary', 'Training Opportunities'

Job dimensions: Actuary

Key: HD – Highly Descriptive,   D – Descriptive,   = In the middle

		HD	D	=	D	HD	
1.	Supervise many		X				No supervision
2.	Teamwork		X				Work independently
3.	Customer contact			X			No customer contact
4.	Work in large organisation		X—	—X			Work alone
5.	Produce goods				X		Provide a service
6.	Fixed salary	X—	—X				Paid by results
7.	Flexitime				X		Fixed hours
8.	Routine work			X—X			Lots of surprises
9.	Lots of travel			X			No travel
10.	Closely managed			X			Managed from afar
11.	Work with same group	X—	—X				Work with different people
12.	Work indoors	X					Work outside
13.	Highly technical		X				Not technical
14.	Little innovation			X			Considerable innovation
15.	Short work cycles			X			Long work projects
16.	Low financial risk	X					High financial risk
17.	High attention to detail	X					Low attention to detail
18.	High specialisation		X				Low specialisation
19.	High visibility				X		Low visibility
20.	Extended working hours			X			9–5 job
21.	Many deadlines			X			Few deadlines
22.	Others depend on you			X			Little dependence
23.	Highly structured	X					Little structure
		HD	D	=	D	HD	

Questionnaire: Management

1. Name and address of organisation

   British Institute of Management, Management House, Cottingham Road, Corby, Northants NN17 1TT

2. Telephone no

   0536 204222

3. Fax no

   0536 201651

4. Typically, for what job(s) does membership of your organisation qualify a person?

   General management – in all organisations

5. Up to what age is it practical for our readers to consider a career change to these occupations?

   Up to 45

6. Minimum education standards necessary

   Degree or equivalent, eg significant senior management experience

7. Qualifying examinations

   —

8. Essential experience

9. Desirable experience

   Combination of several years' general management experience and academic qualifications held

10. Training available (course(s) and examples of existing providers)

    (a) Full-time

    (b) Part-time

    (c) Correspondence course

    (d) Distance learning

    (e) Other

    BIM is a provider of four principal methods of training:

    1. Short training courses of one to three days mainly for management skills
    2. Specifically tailored courses to suit company requirements
    3. Courses linked to qualifications, eg Certificate of management
    4. Training and exposure designed for senior management, eg executive seminars and boardroom briefings

    BIM is a pilot centre for the Accreditation of Prior Learning, a process by which experienced on-the-job competences are assessed against a management qualification

11. Additional comments (government grants and other initiatives for mature students, bursaries, etc)

    Help (financial and time) is provided where appropriate

138

Job dimensions: Office Manager

Key: HD – Highly Descriptive, D – Descriptive, = In the middle

		HD	D	=	D	HD	
1.	Supervise many		X				No supervision
2.	Teamwork		X				Work independently
3.	Customer contact		X				No customer contact
4.	Work in large organisation		X———X				Work alone
5.	Produce goods		X———X				Provide a service
6.	Fixed salary	X					Paid by results
7.	Flexitime					X	Fixed hours
8.	Routine work		X				Lots of surprises
9.	Lots of travel					X	No travel
10.	Closely managed				X		Managed from afar
11.	Work with same group	X					Work with different people
12.	Work indoors	X					Work outside
13.	Highly technical		X———X				Not technical
14.	Little innovation			X			Considerable innovation
15.	Short work cycles		X———X				Long work projects
16.	Low financial risk	X					High financial risk
17.	High attention to detail		X				Low attention to detail
18.	High specialisation		X—X				Low specialisation
19.	High visibility		X				Low visibility
20.	Extended working hours			X———X			9–5 job
21.	Many deadlines		X———X				Few deadlines
22.	Others depend on you	X					Little dependence
23.	Highly structured		X				Little structure
		HD	D	=	D	HD	

Questionnaire: Building Societies

1. Name and address of organisation

    The Chartered Building Societies Institute (CBSI), 19 Baldock Street, Ware, Herts SG12 9DH

2. Telephone no

    0920 465051

3. Fax no

    0920 460016

4. Typically, for what job(s) does membership of your organisation qualify a person?

    Management posts in building societies and allied financial services

5. Up to what age is it practical for our readers to consider a career change to these occupations?

    This obviously varies from society to society and with the nature of the work involved. The scope of building society work has grown enormously since the Building Societies Act 1986 and societies could well be interested in people with specialist knowledge of the new areas into which they are moving

6. Minimum education standards necessary }

    Vary from society to society. For the Associateship four GCSEs and two A levels or relevant experience. (See point 11.) Mature entrants with work experience may gain entry without formal qualifications.

7. Qualifying examinations

    Associateship of the CBSI is the professional qualification. Certificate in Financial Services Practice (CFSP) is also offered. (See point 11.)

8. Essential experience

    Relevant business/financial background

9. Desirable experience

    People-based skills, for dealing with customers, staff, etc

10. Training available (course(s) and examples of existing providers)

    (a) Full-time

    —

    (b) Part-time

    Courses run at some local colleges. CBSI offers starter and refresher courses for both Associateship and CFSP and a correspondence course for the Associateship

    (c) Correspondence course

    (d) Distance learning

    CFSP material is supplied by the Institute

11. Additional comments (government grants and other initiatives for mature students, bursaries, etc)

    Write to the Institute for a copy of 'Building a Career with Building Societies' and the regulations and syllabus. Societies may now be more flexible regarding their recruitment programmes. Clerical staff can study for CFSP for which no educational standards are demanded. Completion of CFSP confers membership of the Institute. A good pass can lead on to the Associateship*

Job dimensions: Building Society Manager

Key: HD – Highly Descriptive, D – Descriptive, = In the middle

		HD	D	=	D	HD	
1.	Supervise many	X					No supervision
2.	Teamwork	X					Work independently
3.	Customer contact	X					No customer contact
4.	Work in large organisation		X———X				Work alone
5.	Produce goods			X			Provide a service
6.	Fixed salary	X					Paid by results
7.	Flexitime				X		Fixed hours
8.	Routine work			X			Lots of surprises
9.	Lots of travel				X		No travel
10.	Closely managed	X					Managed from afar
11.	Work with same group	X					Work with different people
12.	Work indoors	X					Work outside
13.	Highly technical			X			Not technical
14.	Little innovation					X	Considerable innovation
15.	Short work cycles		X				Long work projects
16.	Low financial risk		X				High financial risk
17.	High attention to detail		X				Low attention to detail
18.	High specialisation			X			Low specialisation
19.	High visibility	X					Low visibility
20.	Extended working hours		X				9–5 job
21.	Many deadlines			X			Few deadlines
22.	Others depend on you		X				Little dependence
23.	Highly structured	X					Little structure
		HD	D	=	D	HD	

---

* Building society mergers and rationalisation have led to the closure of branches and consequent redundancies.

Questionnaire: Chartered Secretary/Administrator

1. Name and address of organisation

   The Institute of Chartered Secretaries and Administrators (ICSA), 16 Park Crescent, London W1N 4AH

2. Telephone no

   071-580 4741

3. Fax no

   071-323 1132

4. Typically, for what job(s) does membership of your organisation qualify a person?

   Opportunities in company secretarial work, administration and management related to finance, law, personnel and data administration and general administration

5. Up to what age is it practical for our readers to consider a career change to these occupations?

   35–45 approximately

6. Minimum education standards necessary

   Entry possible with no qualifications. Exemptions given with HNC/HND, degree or professional qualification

7. Qualifying examinations

   Foundation, Pre-professional, Professional

8. Essential experience

   —

9. Desirable experience

   Background in administration, finance, law, IT, personnel or management

10. Training available (course(s) and examples of existing providers)

    Financial administration, pension fund administration, company secretarial administration and management, local government administration

    (a) Full-time

    Humberside College of Higher Education

    (b) Part-time

    City of London Polytechnic

    (c) Correspondence course

    Rapid Results College

    (d) Distance learning

    Colchester Institute

    (e) Other

    —

11. Additional comments (government grants and other initiatives for mature students, bursaries, etc)

    —

Job dimensions: Company Secretary

Key: HD – Highly Descriptive, D – Descriptive, = In the middle

		HD	D	=	D	HD	
1.	Supervise many		X		X		No supervision
2.	Teamwork		X				Work independently
3.	Customer contact					X	No customer contact
4.	Work in large organisation			X			Work alone
5.	Produce goods					X	Provide a service
6.	Fixed salary	X					Paid by results
7.	Flexitime					X	Fixed hours
8.	Routine work	X					Lots of surprises
9.	Lots of travel					X	No travel
10.	Closely managed			X			Managed from afar
11.	Work with same group	X					Work with different people
12.	Work indoors	X					Work outside
13.	Highly technical		X				Not technical
14.	Little innovation	X					Considerable innovation
15.	Short work cycles		X		X		Long work projects
16.	Low financial risk	X					High financial risk
17.	High attention to detail	X					Low attention to detail
18.	High specialisation	X					Low specialisation
19.	High visibility			X			Low visibility
20.	Extended working hours				X		9–5 job
21.	Many deadlines		X				Few deadlines
22.	Others depend on you		X				Little dependence
23.	Highly structured		X				Little structure
		HD	D	=	D	HD	

Hairdressing and Beauty Care

Young people on Youth Training (YT) comprise the bulk of new entrants to the profession.

A number of courses are run throughout the country on a full-time basis for a new joint Hairdressing Board/City and Guilds qualification. Other colleges offer their own awards. If you are prepared to pay an expensive fee, you can attend an intensive course at a private school and receive an 'in-house' certificate. On a more practical basis, it is worthwhile taking a look at the requirements for sponsorship under the Employment Training (ET) scheme described in Chapter 7. If you are eligible you can participate in a programme which will give you practical experience in cutting, colouring processes, blow drying, perming and styling. You will also learn about reception duties and how to deal with customers, as well as 'behind the scenes' duties such as ordering stock, maintaining records and helping with accounts. Most of the work will be in local salons and will include long periods of standing. Such a course could be invaluable to a married woman returning to work – both as a 'refresher' and as a prelude to buying a business.

Consult *Careers in Hairdressing and Beauty Therapy* by Alexa Stace (Kogan Page) for further advice.

We sought the views of a hairdresser who has had 25 years' experience in the business. She said: 'I do not find the standing too tiring unless we have a very hot summer. I have a genuine interest in people and love discussing topics which we can share – like a love of gardening. I get lots of useful hints! There is tremendous job satisfaction to be obtained from making customers feel better and happier after a visit to their hairdresser, especially if they have been ill or depressed – it's a tonic for them.'

Here are success stories of Employment Training in hairdressing from the Guildford College of Technology:

Shelagh, 50, a retired social worker, wished to train as a hairdresser and beauty therapist. A placement was arranged with a local salon which offered her employment at the end of the 12 months' training period. She pursued a City and Guilds in Hairdressing at Guildford College and also took part-time courses in beauty therapy at Farnborough College.

Susan did a refresher hairdressing course after working for two years in the retail trade. Her employment placement was with a Guildford hairdresser and later she chose to become self-employed.

Questionnaire: Hairdressing

1. Name and address of organisation

   The Hairdressing Council, 12 David House, 45 High Street, London SE25 6HJ

2. Telephone no

   081-771 6205

3. Fax no

   —

4. Typically, for what job(s) does membership of your organisation qualify a person?

   The Council will register all hairdressers who are suitably qualified

5. Up to what age is it practical for our readers to consider a career change to these occupations?

   Any age

6. Minimum education standards necessary to become registered

   —

7. Qualifying examinations

   City and Guilds

8. Essential experience

   Three years in a salon is needed for an apprenticeship

9. Desirable experience

   —

10. Training available (course(s) and examples of existing providers)

    City and Guilds taken at college

    (a) Full-time

    —

    (b) Part-time

    —

    (c) Correspondence course

    —

    (d) Distance learning

    —

    (e) Other

    Hairdressing colleges

11. Additional comments (government grants and other initiatives for mature students, bursaries, etc)

    At present anyone can become a hairdresser without any training. The Council objects to this. It receives many calls from members of the public who have had their hair damaged by untrained hairdressers. It is not fair on the fully trained hairdresser that such people are allowed to practise, use dangerous chemicals and even train others themselves

Job dimensions: Hairdresser

Key: HD – Highly Descriptive, D – Descriptive, = In the middle

		HD	D	=	D	HD	
1.	Supervise many			X			No supervision
2.	Teamwork		X				Work independently
3.	Customer contact	X					No customer contact
4.	Work in large organisation		X				Work alone
5.	Produce goods					X	Provide a service
6.	Fixed salary					X	Paid by results
7.	Flexitime		X——→X				Fixed hours
8.	Routine work		X				Lots of surprises
9.	Lots of travel					X	No travel
10.	Closely managed		X				Managed from afar
11.	Work with same group		X				Work with different people
12.	Work indoors	X					Work outside
13.	Highly technical			X			Not technical
14.	Little innovation		X——→X				Considerable innovation
15.	Short work cycles	X					Long work projects
16.	Low financial risk	X					High financial risk
17.	High attention to detail		X				Low attention to detail
18.	High specialisation			X			Low specialisation
19.	High visibility	X					Low visibility
20.	Extended working hours		X——→X				9–5 job
21.	Many deadlines		X				Few deadlines
22.	Others depend on you	X					Little dependence
23.	Highly structured					X	Little structure
		HD	D	=	D	HD	

Questionnaire: Insurance

1. Name and address of organisation	The Chartered Insurance Institute (CII), 20 Aldermanbury, London EC2V 7HY
2. Telephone no	071-606 3835
3. Typically, for what job(s) does membership of your organisation qualify a person?	All professional posts, eg underwriting, claims, surveying, broking, sales/marketing
4. Up to what age is it practical for our readers to consider a career change to these occupations?	For some posts, eg sales, maturity can be an advantage. For others, entry becomes more difficult, but not impossible after 27–28 years of age
5. Minimum education standards necessary	Over the age of 25 no entrance qualifications stipulated
6. Qualifying examinations	Associateship and Fellowship of the Chartered Insurance Institute
7. Essential experience	Minimum three years' approved experience required for attainment of FCII as from 1992
8. Desirable experience	Other financial, service industry experience
9. Training available (course(s) and examples of existing providers)	
(a) Full-time	ACII available at CII College of Insurance, Sevenoaks
(b) Part-time	Widely available at colleges throughout the UK
(c) Correspondence course } (d) Distance learning }	Provided by CII tuition service
(e) Other	Insurance subjects available in number of full-time higher education courses and as options within BTEC courses
10. Additional comments (government grants and other initiatives for mature students, bursaries, etc)	New examination structure and syllabus were introduced with first examinations April 1992. Other CII courses available – Certificate of Proficiency, Financial Planning Certificate

147

Questionnaire: Insurance Brokers

1. Name and address of organisation

British Insurance and Investment Brokers Association (BIIBA), BIIBA House, 14 Bevis Marks, London EC3A 7NT

2. Telephone no

071-623 9043

3. Fax no

071-626 9676

4. Typically, for what job(s) does membership of your organisation qualify a person?

Membership of the Association does not qualify you for a particular job. Our members are insurance brokers, investment brokers, and independent financial advisers

5. Up to what age is it practical for our readers to consider a career change to these occupations?

No upper age limit

6. Minimum education standards necessary

Typically A levels, BTEC or degree. It is an industry, however, where personality and communication skills can circumvent formal qualifications

7. Qualifying examinations

—

8. Essential experience

—

9. Desirable experience

Banking or other areas of insurance. Good communications skills

10. Training available (course(s) and examples of existing providers)

Most training is on the job. However, many firms encourage people to study for the Chartered Insurance Institute exams. BIIBA runs a wide range of one-day technical courses

11. Additional comments (government grants and other initiatives for mature students, bursaries, etc)

BIIBA runs a YT scheme for the industry, which it hopes to open up to more mature students

Job dimensions: Insurance Broker

Key: HD - Highly Descriptive, D - Descriptive, = In the middle

		HD	D	=	D	HD	
1.	Supervise many		X				No supervision
2.	Teamwork		X				Work independently
3.	Customer contact	X					No customer contact
4.	Work in large organisation			X			Work alone
5.	Produce goods				X		Provide a service
6.	Fixed salary			X—X			Paid by results
7.	Flexitime				X		Fixed hours
8.	Routine work			X			Lots of surprises
9.	Lots of travel				X		No travel
10.	Closely managed			X			Managed from afar
11.	Work with same group		X				Work with different people
12.	Work indoors		X				Work outside
13.	Highly technical			X			Not technical
14.	Little innovation	X					Considerable innovation
15.	Short work cycles		X				Long work projects
16.	Low financial risk			X			High financial risk
17.	High attention to detail		X				Low attention to detail
18.	High specialisation			X			Low specialisation
19.	High visibility			X			Low visibility
20.	Extended working hours				X		9–5 job
21.	Many deadlines		X				Few deadlines
22.	Others depend on you		X				Little dependence
23.	Highly structured		X				Little structure
		HD	D	=	D	HD	

Public Relations

Public relations is a management function, charged with the responsibility of managing an organisation's reputation – shaping, protecting and promoting it.

There are two distinct types of public relations operation:

1. the in-house public relations department of an organisation, which can originate and implement the public relations policies suitable for that particular company or institution, and
2. the public relations consultancy, which can be either an individual or a group of external specialists drawing on his/its own experience and expertise to provide advisory and implementation services to a variety of client organisations.

The number of people working in public relations in the UK has been estimated at around 19,000. The rate of growth in the number of public relations jobs at all levels has probably been higher than that of any other management function over the past 15 years.

Questionnaire: Public Relations

1. Name and address of organisation

    The Institute of Public Relations, The Old Trading House, 15 Northburgh Street, London EC1V 0PR

2. Telephone no

    071-253 5151

3. Fax no

    071-490 0588

4. Typically, for what job(s) does membership of your organisation qualify a person?

    Public relations practitioner

5. Up to what age is it practical for our readers to consider a career change to these occupations?

    30–35

6. Minimum education standards necessary

    Graduate or specific work experience, eg financial, hi-tech

7. Qualifying examinations

    Three first degree courses, CAM Diploma (see below)

8. Essential experience

9. Desirable experience

10. Training available (course(s) and examples of existing providers) }

    Three first degrees, MSc in PR

    (a) Full-time

    (b) Part-time

    CAM Certificate and Diploma (see below)

    (c) Correspondence course

    —

    (d) Distance learning

    MSc from Stirling University, CAM Diploma

    (e) Other

    —

11. Additional comments (government grants and other initiatives for mature students, bursaries, etc)

    Twenty-three colleges of further education and polytechnics teach the Communication, Advertising and Marketing Education Foundation (CAM) Certificate and Diploma syllabuses. Certain charities take volunteer trainees on an 'expenses only' basis to gain hands-on experience. Further details are available from the Institute

151

Job dimensions: Public Relations Officer

Key: HD – Highly Descriptive,   D – Descriptive,   = In the middle

		HD	D	=	D	HD	
1.	Supervise many				X		No supervision
2.	Teamwork	X		X			Work independently
3.	Customer contact	X					No customer contact
4.	Work in large organisation		X	X			Work alone
5.	Produce goods					X	Provide a service
6.	Fixed salary	X	X				Paid by results
7.	Flexitime				X		Fixed hours
8.	Routine work		X	X			Lots of surprises
9.	Lots of travel		X				No travel
10.	Closely managed				X		Managed from afar
11.	Work with same group		X				Work with different people
12.	Work indoors	X					Work outside
13.	Highly technical				X		Not technical
14.	Little innovation				X	X	Considerable innovation
15.	Short work cycles		X	X			Long work projects
16.	Low financial risk		X				High financial risk
17.	High attention to detail		X				Low attention to detail
18.	High specialisation			X			Low specialisation
19.	High visibility	X					Low visibility
20.	Extended working hours		X				9–5 job
21.	Many deadlines	X					Few deadlines
22.	Others depend on you		X				Little dependence
23.	Highly structured				X		Little structure
		HD	D	=	D	HD	

Purchasing and Supply

The Institute of Purchasing and Supply
The Institute has about 19,000 corporate members, associates and students and is the largest professional purchasing and supply organisation in Europe.

Managing and operating the supply chain. IPS members hold appointments in most sectors of industry, commerce and the public service; they manage the expenditure of many billions of pounds annually on goods and services.

Role of the IPS. It is the Institute's principal objective to make as effective as possible the contribution to the economy of the purchasing and supply function.

The IPS Professional Examinations Scheme. This provides a thorough grounding in business studies (including economics, quantitative studies, finance, law and management principles) as well as studies of specialist purchasing and supply subjects. Over 100 educational establishments in the UK offer block-release, part-time and full-time courses leading to the IPS Professional Examinations Scheme.

The Certificates in Purchasing and Stores offer an opportunity for those working in purchasing departments, stores and warehouses, who do not have the two A-level entry qualifications required by the IPS, to obtain a recognised qualification.

Training is largely on the job. You can expect to develop the following personal qualities, skills and knowledge as your career progresses:

- *Decision-making skills.* The buyer has to take responsibility for his purchasing decisions.
- *Communication skills.* There is a great deal of personal contact, both on the phone and face to face. Letters must be precise.
- *Analytical skills.* Much of the necessary data collected will be numerical, so basic numeracy skills are important.
- *Finance and law.* The buyer has to acquire a knowledge of the laws of contract and sale of goods. The financial stability of suppliers must be investigated.
- *Management skills.* Planning, organisation, control and motivation are the stock-in-trade of the good buyer.
- *Computer systems.* These have become the norm by which purchasing and stores procedures are operated.

If you have the mental and emotional resilience, you can train for a responsible, varied and satisfying career with excellent prospects.

Case study

A graduate was sponsored by an engine manufacturer for a degree in business studies. After graduation he worked for his sponsors and rose quickly to the rank of chief buyer. He then joined a boiler manufacturer as materials manager and later moved to a motor manufacturer as senior buyer. The next switch was to an engineering conglomerate as divisional director of purchasing and supply with responsibility for supply management in 22 operating companies. He was selected for a new management team to bring an ailing operating division back into profitability. His role was to create an effective materials management structure. Finally, he became a director of a marketing firm involved in commodities purchasing and the money market.

Questionnaire: Purchasing and Supply

1. Name and address of organisation

Institute of Purchasing and Supply (IPS), Easton House, Easton on the Hill, Stamford, Lincs PE9 3NZ

2. Telephone no

0780 56777

3. Fax no

0780 51610

4. Typically, for what job(s) does membership of your organisation qualify a person?

Purchasing, supply, inventory control, stores management, materials management, project and contracts management, logistics, physical distribution management

5. Up to what age is it practical for our readers to consider a career change to these occupations?

50 (depending on level at which transfer takes place)

6. Minimum education standards necessary

Two A levels or equivalent for those under 23

7. Qualifying examinations

Institute of Purchasing and Supply professional examinations and Association of Supervisors in Purchasing and Supply supervisory examinations

8. Essential experience

Three years in purchasing and supply for professional qualifications

9. Desirable experience

—

10. Training available (course(s) and examples of existing providers)

Available at over 100 colleges. (Send to IPS for college list.)

   (a) Full-time

   (b) Part-time

Yes

   (c) Correspondence course

Available from three colleges (See college list.)

   (d) Distance learning

IPS scheme being developed

   (e) Other

Practical training courses (short duration) run by IPS and other organisations

11. Additional comments (government grants and other initiatives for mature students, bursaries, etc)

—

155

Job dimensions: Purchasing Officer

Key: HD – Highly Descriptive, D – Descriptive, = In the middle

		HD	D	=	D	HD	
1.	Supervise many				X		No supervision
2.	Teamwork		X				Work independently
3.	Customer contact	X					No customer contact
4.	Work in large organisation		X—X				Work alone
5.	Produce goods					X	Provide a service
6.	Fixed salary	X					Paid by results
7.	Flexitime					X	Fixed hours
8.	Routine work		X				Lots of surprises
9.	Lots of travel				X		No travel
10.	Closely managed		X				Managed from afar
11.	Work with same group		X				Work with different people
12.	Work indoors		X				Work outside
13.	Highly technical			X—X			Not technical
14.	Little innovation		X				Considerable innovation
15.	Short work cycles		X———X				Long work projects
16.	Low financial risk	X					High financial risk
17.	High attention to detail		X				Low attention to detail
18.	High specialisation				X		Low specialisation
19.	High visibility				X		Low visibility
20.	Extended working hours					X	9–5 job
21.	Many deadlines	X					Few deadlines
22.	Others depend on you	X					Little dependence
23.	Highly structured		X				Little structure
		HD	D	=	D	HD	

Questionnaire: Sales and Marketing Management

1. Name and address of organisation

   Institute of Sales and Marketing Management, 31 Upper George Street, Luton, Beds LU1 2RD

2. Telephone no

   0582 411130

3. Fax no

   0582 453640

4. Typically, for what job(s) does membership of your organisation qualify a person?

   Selling, sales management

5. Up to what age is it practical for our readers to consider a career change to these occupations?

   At any age, provided the person has drive

6. Minimum education standards necessary

   Life skills, numeracy, literacy; interpersonal skills and vocational experience

7. Qualifying examinations

   See point 11

8. Essential experience

   Vocational experience

9. Desirable experience

   Sales and customer liaison

10. Training available (course(s) and examples of existing providers)

    See point 11

    (a) Full-time

    (b) Part-time

    (c) Correspondence course
    (d) Distance learning

    Via the ISMM Education Division

    (e) Other

    —

11. Additional comments (government grants and other initiatives for mature students, bursaries, etc)

    The ISMM is an examining body and sets training standards. It can provide a list of approved training organisations from which to make the final choice.

    The ISMM insists that planned training (as distinct from education) forms an integral part of a salesperson's career development

157

Job dimensions: Sales Manager

Key: HD – Highly Descriptive,   D – Descriptive,   = In the middle

		HD	D	=	D	HD	
1.	Supervise many	X					No supervision
2.	Teamwork	X					Work independently
3.	Customer contact	X					No customer contact
4.	Work in large organisation		X	X			Work alone
5.	Produce goods					X	Provide a service
6.	Fixed salary					X	Paid by results
7.	Flexitime	X					Fixed hours
8.	Routine work		X	X			Lots of surprises
9.	Lots of travel		X				No travel
10.	Closely managed		X				Managed from afar
11.	Work with same group		X				Work with different people
12.	Work indoors		X		X		Work outside
13.	Highly technical		X		X		Not technical
14.	Little innovation				X		Considerable innovation
15.	Short work cycles		X				Long work projects
16.	Low financial risk				X		High financial risk
17.	High attention to detail		X	X			Low attention to detail
18.	High specialisation		X		X		Low specialisation
19.	High visibility	X					Low visibility
20.	Extended working hours		X				9–5 job
21.	Many deadlines		X				Few deadlines
22.	Others depend on you		X				Little dependence
23.	Highly structured				X		Little structure
		HD	D	=	D	HD	

Questionnaire: Solicitor

1. Name and address of organisation

The Law Society, 227–228 Strand, London WC2R 1BA

2. Telephone no

071-242 1222

3. Fax no

071-583 5531

4. Typically, for what job(s) does membership of your organisation qualify a person?

Solicitor

5. Up to what age is it practical for our readers to consider a career change to these occupations?

Difficult to say. Some people qualify as solicitors in their late 30s/early 40s. After that they may have problems but it would depend on their background and experience

6. Minimum education standards necessary

Normally degree or equivalent but provision made for non-degree entrants

7. Qualifying examinations

8. Essential experience

9. Desirable experience

Academic stage, normally common professional examination, or law degree, followed by Legal Practice Course. Two-year training contract including Professional Skills course

10. Training available (course(s) and examples of existing providers)

(a) Full-time

(b) Part-time

Yes

(c) Correspondence course

Yes, at degree level

(d) Distance learning

Yes

(e) Other

—

11. Additional comments (government grants and other initiatives for mature students, bursaries, etc)

Some local authority grants available. Otherwise bank loans, sponsorship, some bursaries. Write to Careers Promotions Officer of the Law Society for their brochure 'Solicitors – A Career for Tomorrow' which includes interesting case histories

Non-graduates can qualify as solicitors by training through the Institute of Legal Executives while in relevant employment. Further information from the Institute of Legal Executives, Kempston Manor, Kempston, Bedford MK42 7AB

Job dimensions: Solicitor

Key: HD – Highly Descriptive, D – Descriptive, = In the middle

		HD	D	=	D	HD	
1.	Supervise many		X———X				No supervision
2.	Teamwork		X———X				Work independently
3.	Customer contact	X					No customer contact
4.	Work in large organisation			X			Work alone
5.	Produce goods					X	Provide a service
6.	Fixed salary	X					Paid by results
7.	Flexitime			X			Fixed hours
8.	Routine work			X			Lots of surprises
9.	Lots of travel			X			No travel
10.	Closely managed			X			Managed from afar
11.	Work with same group				X		Work with different people
12.	Work indoors	X					Work outside
13.	Highly technical		X				Not technical
14.	Little innovation			X			Considerable innovation
15.	Short work cycles		X				Long work projects
16.	Low financial risk	X					High financial risk
17.	High attention to detail	X					Low attention to detail
18.	High specialisation		X				Low specialisation
19.	High visibility	X					Low visibility
20.	Extended working hours		X				9–5 job
21.	Many deadlines		X				Few deadlines
22.	Others depend on you	X					Little dependence
23.	Highly structured			X			Little structure
		HD	D	=	D	HD	

The Careers Centre

We have tried to cover a wide range of job opportunities but there is not enough space to cover every possibility. The Careers Centre produces a careers pack for over 400 different types of job ranging from accountant to zookeeper. Each career pack contains a job description, personal qualities required, entry qualifications, prospects for future development, age limits, etc. All information is updated three times a year. Contact the Careers Centre, Scottish Executive Centre, McIver House, Cadogan Street, Glasgow G2 7HF for their brochure.

Chapter 7
Training

Do not let the lack of formal educational qualifications deter you from achieving your goal. George Carey is the son of a hospital porter. He went to a secondary modern school and left with no O levels. He did his national service as a wireless operator in the RAF. During this period he educated himself, and after demobilisation he began his training. In April 1991 George Carey was enthroned as the Archbishop of Canterbury.

You should by now have identified your own sphere of job interest or potential areas of self-employment. Do not be deterred from pursuing your ambitions because you:

(a) feel you lack the necessary skills or qualifications;
(b) lack funds;
(c) need to retrain or update skills, or
(d) are restrained or hampered by family commitments.

There are ways and means to overcome or circumvent most of these obstacles. Advice and counselling are obtainable from Adult Guidance Agencies and the Careers Service. A discussion with a careers officer will help to define your training target. A wide range of educational and training opportunities is available to you. Learning systems are both flexible and accessible – full time, part time, distance learning and permutations within these headings. For certain careers, employers will give you a job and subsidise your training while you qualify. Some examples are given on page 166.

Further education colleges

Local education authorities run over 300 colleges of further education. Courses cover commercial, technical and vocational subjects. Your nearest education centre will keep your local library well supplied with literature, especially in early September which is the peak time for enrolment.

Commercial subjects include accounting, business studies, computers/information technology, economics, languages, shorthand, typewriting and word-processing. Technical and vocational subjects include bricklaying, chemistry, electronics, hairdressing, plumbing and tailoring. The range is virtually limitless. There are full-time courses, part-time courses up to 21 hours a week, and evening classes. The figure of 21 hours is of particular significance. The Department of Social Security will allow unemployed people to study for up to 21 hours a week without losing benefit. There are rules attached, such as remaining available for work if it comes up, but don't let this deter you. Some colleges, especially in areas of high unemployment, are geared to switch you to an evening class if you are found suitable work. Other colleges allow you to build up credits if the work is seasonal.

Discuss any problems with the college's administrators, who will be keen to help. Large colleges have counselling staff. Keep the Unemployment Benefit Office in the picture. Don't undervalue your capabilities – remember that if you achieve 40 per cent in an A-level examination you should get a D or E grade pass! (The pass mark varies annually according to the subject and the standard of the papers set.) If you are unemployed, you will, at least, get a substantial discount off the fees, depending on local rules.

Universities

You may have noticed several changes taking place in third level education. Previously the fundamental difference between a university and a polytechnic was that a university had the power to award degrees at its own discretion. Polytechnics, on the other hand, had their degrees awarded by the Council for National Academic Awards (CNAA). The CNAA has now been abolished and all polytechnics have been given university status. At the time of going to press, most have changed their names to reflect this but a few have yet to agree satisfactory new titles.

Full-time courses

If you are 21 or over, universities recognise and welcome you as a mature student. One in seven new university students is 21 or older. A mature candidate does not have to comply with the same entry requirements as school-leavers. Your qualifications and work experience will be taken into account. Mature students are often more highly motivated and achieve better results than younger entrants.

The majority of universities have child-care facilities and can help with finding accommodation.

Half a million people enrol each year on short courses ranging from a few

163

weeks to nine months. Contact your local university to see what is on offer. The average length of a full-time degree course is three years. Send a *postcard* to the Registrar of any university you are interested in and quote the particular course prospectus you require. If you have a degree which is no longer relevant to the career change you have in mind, you may consider taking a Master's degree.

Part-time courses

Many Master's degrees are now operated on a modular system to enable study for a few weeks at a time so as to earn credits, which contribute ultimately to the awarding of a degree.

Universities are increasingly geared to meet the needs of mature students who want to study locally, and those who work full time and wish to update their skills as part of their job search programme. Consult your nearest university for details of their part-time courses. For those who work in London, Birkbeck College has a well-deserved reputation with mature students for its part-time degree courses. Much teaching takes place in the evenings. Goldsmiths' College also offers part-time degree and diploma courses.

External students

The University of London has a scheme for external students to enable all or most of the studying to be done at home. For details, send a postcard to the Secretary for External Students, The University of London, Senate House, Malet Street, London WC1E 7HU.

Qualifications

If you do not have the standard minimum entrance requirements for a degree course (GCE A/AS qualifications or equivalent), universities have special procedures to process applications from mature students. You can take an A/AS examination after preparing yourself by attending evening classes at your local college of further education. Consult your local college. You may be advised to take an Access course particularly designed for mature students.

For further details apply for the leaflet 'University Entrance – Mature Students' by sending a postcard to UCCA, PO Box 28, Cheltenham, Glos GL50 3SA.

Finance – Full-time degree course

If you are offered a place at a university for a full-time first degree course, you should be eligible for a mandatory award. This is intended to cover university fees and a grant towards maintenance. The government has now frozen the level of the maintenance grant but loan facilities are available for students up to the age of 50 to top-up the grant.

Ask your Careers Service for a copy of the booklet 'Grants to Students'. If you fail to get a mandatory grant, some local education authorities may consider you for a discretionary award.

Alas, there are no awards for part-time degree courses. If you prefer to study part time and the course will enhance your value to your present employer, you may be able to get financial help with the fees.

The Open University (OU)

Over a million people have taken OU courses which are specifically designed for those who have had little or no previous academic work experience. Half the applicants do not have the normal entry requirements for a degree course. You can study on a part-time basis for a degree and by distance learning on non-degree courses. The OU's learning packages are mailed to your home. Back-up is provided by TV programmes, videos and audio cassettes, supplemented by summer schools. OU degrees have exactly the same graduate status as any other degree awarded by a British university. Those wanting to go in for management should ask for details from the Open Business School. To get a copy of 'Open Opportunities', write to the Central Enquiry Service, The Open University, Walton Hall, PO Box 71, Milton Keynes MK7 6AA.

The Open College

This national organisation provides study packages for home study. No qualifications are required for anyone willing to start at Foundation level. The range of courses embraces information technology, craft skills, salesmanship, plant operating and preparation for City and Guilds type examinations. Write to the Open College, Freepost, PO Box 35, Abingdon, Oxon OX14 34BR for the free guide to courses entitled the 'Open Book'.

(The term 'Open College' is also used by colleges to indicate the availability of courses in subjects specifically aimed at adults.)

165

Colleges of higher education

Unlike universities these institutions are funded by local education authorities, and entry requirements are more flexible.

Mature students can study on a full- or part-time basis at these institutions. Many also run sandwich courses. Advice about the range of courses can be obtained from your Careers Office or from the Admissions Officer at the college of your choice.

Correspondence courses/distance learning

Many people in senior management posts obtained their accountancy and salesmanship professional qualifications by studying for examinations by means of correspondence courses. It is a tough, lonely method but, if you use a reputable correspondence college, it is an effective way of getting through examinations. Recent innovations using new technology have been introduced by many correspondence colleges under the title of distance learning. Tapes – audio and video – have made courses more interesting, and computerised marking has speeded the question and answer process. Warwick Business School has a distance learning Master of Business Administration programme to allow people to study while holding down a full-time job or coping with other commitments. Contact Distance Learning MBA Office, Warwick Business School, University of Warwick, Coventry CV4 7AL; 0203 524100.

One of the country's leading open learning providers is the National Extension College; 6000 students enrol annually for over 80 courses. Recent developments have been courses in the new GCSE subjects with a growing number of business and vocational topics such as accounting, data-processing and editing. The NEC trains over 3000 British Telecom technicians annually in the largest open learning scheme outside the Open University. Write to the Customer Services Department, National Extension College, 18 Brooklands Avenue, Cambridge CB2 2HN.

Training sponsored by employers

From Chapter 6 we have extracted some examples of training sponsored by employers.

Civil Service (page 52)

  (a) Information technology. Training given, including help towards qualifying for membership of the British Computer Society.

(b) Accountancy. Executive Officers are able to apply for training for a professional qualification.
(c) Surveyors. Impressive training programme.
(d) Probation officers. Three hundred students each year are sponsored on professional courses.

Local Government (page 65)
Day release granted for qualification training as well as training while doing the job.

Religion – Christian (page 90)
Recommended candidates are eligible for grants.

Libraries (page 62)
Many mature students study part time with support from employers.

Health Service (page 70)
(a) Chiropody. Grants mandatory dependent upon the individual.
(b) Radiographers. Department of Health bursaries available.
(c) Occupational therapists. Regional Health Authority bursaries available on attainment of place on full-time course.

Social Work (page 93)
The CCETSW will send details of discretionary awards which may be available from local education authorities.

Plumbing (page 110)
Plumbing is one of the courses available under Employment Training.

Motor Industry (page 108)
Grants are available from companies in the industry.

Accountancy (page 131)
You may enter a 'training contract' with a firm which will provide your training; you agree to work for the benefit of the firm. (See also pages 55 and 66 and Civil Service above.)

Civil Engineering (page 98)
A scholarship scheme is available to supplement LEA grants.

Solicitor (page 159)
Some LEA grants are available.

Many employers recruit mature staff as management trainees. One leading retailer advertises for people holding supervisory positions in another commercial environment and offers an excellent training programme. One local authority invites applicants concerned about the environment to apply for a post as trainee Environmental Health Officer, which is linked to a four-year honours degree sandwich course at the University of London.

On the technical side, British Telecom has launched an apprenticeship scheme for people up to the age of 41. Peugeot Talbot has taken on apprentices, between the ages of 25 and 33, from its existing staff to be trained for three years in electrical craftwork. The employers will continue to pay the same wages.

Your local Careers Officer will be able to advise you about training opportunities with employers in your own locality, and your own study of careers reference books in the library will turn up others.

Case studies

Kate was a library assistant. She took the OU course in mathematics and computers. After completion, she found a job in computer programming and her income has now increased sevenfold.

Surrey County Council introduced a mature graduate entry scheme to train graduates as teachers in shortage subject disciplines. Today a former priest, geologist, company director and marketing executive are teaching respectively mathematics, physics, design and business studies.

A professional footballer knows that at the age of 36 his soccer career is nearly over. A few years ago he began studying with the OU. He now has his BA degree and is ready to start as a teacher when he hangs up his boots.

There are countless ways to train and educate yourself further. Use the formal facilities of Adult Guidance Agencies and consult informally the staff of colleges and training institutions. You may be able to use the Employment Training scheme. If you decide to launch your own business, you may qualify for the Enterprise Support Scheme (see page 174).

Recommended reading

Second Chances: The Guide to Adult Education and Training Opportunities, Andrew

Pates and Martin Good, published by the Careers and Occupational Information Centre (COIC).

Once you have identified the course you want, you can also refer to *The Kogan Page Mature Student's Handbook* by Margaret Korving, published by Kogan Page, which groups colleges in geographical areas.

Both books should be in reference libraries and careers offices.

The Careers Service/Adult Guidance Agencies

Many readers will have used the Careers Service when it was directed mainly at school-leavers. Today this situation is changing.

Careers officers are employed by local education authorities with statutory responsibilities for school-leavers up to the age of 18–19 (A levels). However, many authorities are now expanding their client services and are seeking revenue-earning contracts from Training and Enterprise Councils (TECs). As a result some Careers Service offices now offer an 'all age' guidance service. If you are a mature job seeker, you have no right to *demand* a service, but in most areas you will be allowed to browse through their extensive library services, provided you don't draw upon their resources. Everything depends upon the county in which you live.

Ring up your County Council and ask about its Adult Guidance Agencies (AGAs) or Educational Guidance Services. Unemployed people may be referred to the AGAs by Jobcentres in their capacity as training agents for the Training Agency. Other adults, not classed as unemployed, may be married women seeking further education possibilities.

Some counties operate on a questionnaire basis to save Careers Officers' time. The enquirer is given an appointment after filling in a questionnaire. Your local Jobcentre will know the basis on which your area Career Service operates, and whether you are eligible for consideration for the Employment Training (ET) scheme. The Careers Officer will assess your likes and dislikes, so readers who have completed the exercises in Chapter 5 should be well prepared. No Careers Officer will tell you what to do. He or she will help you to think through your problems logically, by listening and discussing them with you. An interview usually lasts about one and a half hours. The arrangement is open-ended so that a client can ask for a further, follow-up interview.

Clients may be recommended to join Access courses to bring themselves up to A-level standard. Such courses will include assertiveness training and role-playing to help bolster self-esteem. If you have a degree, most counties have a Graduate Careers Advisory Service. Your Careers Officer provides a local response to local needs. He or she will suggest various options to clients. Careers Officers liaise closely with local employers and, by giving talks to Rotary Clubs and similar organisations, they receive useful feedback.

A Careers Officer told us that many people are inclined to undersell themselves. The confidence of married women returners to cope with a new job is often minimal. They are encouraged to recognise their own worth and to appreciate that they can transfer their experience and skills to other situations positively. How difficult it is to break into the job market depends upon local market forces but persevere – you may be pleasantly surprised. Careers Officers find much satisfaction in helping clients to bring a new dimension to their lives. (Those interested in training as a Careers Officer should ask for the Local Government Training Board leaflet referred to on page 60. Mature students with relevant work experience, but without a degree, will be considered for the one-year training course.) One married woman returner was urged to take her A levels which she did successfully. She is now embarked on a career as a teacher in a junior school.

We spoke to an Adult Guidance Agency in one area. The county council, under whose auspices it operates, responded successfully to a tender and the Agency now acts as a training agent to ET. In areas of high unemployment, such as Liverpool, candidates may have to wait six months to secure a place on a relevant training course. Places on ET are directly dependent on specific local job vacancies or self-employment opportunities being available on completion of training. Because of stringent funding arrangements, county boundaries have become borders to ensure that training takes place within the county which receives funding from the Agency.

The general conclusion from our discussions is that ET is now beginning to stabilise. It received bad publicity a few years ago when the government cracked down on people drawing unemployment benefit and working unofficially in the black economy. The result was that professional scroungers were made unwilling conscripts into training programmes and caused havoc. The situation has now corrected itself. For years, employers enjoyed a steady flow of school-leavers willing to work for basic wages. That is no longer the case. Employers are now becoming more receptive to the idea of engaging mature workers and, thankfully, job advertisements with upper age limits are becoming increasingly rare. Job seekers with the determination to retrain and re-equip themselves will now meet with a more favourable response.

Employment Training

'If the only thing stopping you getting a job is training, the only thing stopping you training is you.' ET slogan

Employment Training (ET) is mainly intended for those who have been out of work for over six months. But the rules are flexible so do not let this official guideline prevent you from making an application. Those returning to the labour market after a break because of family responsibilities, and ex-regular members of HM forces, need only to be out of work to be eligible. The six-month rule will not apply where people join the programme for training to start their own business or to train in a skill to meet a local labour market shortage.

The training itself, as well as the period spent with an employer on placement, will cost you nothing. If you are unemployed, you will continue to receive your usual benefits. Everyone who joins ET receives a weekly training allowance of £10 plus any money spent on fares over £5 a week. Ask at the Jobcentre for details of the current financial arrangements – they are frequently revised. You may even get a Training Bonus on completion of your training! Training can take between 3 and 12 months and will be designed to meet your personal needs and prepare you for the job for which you are aiming. Your training agent will help you to make up your mind about the course for which you are best suited.

Large employers are co-operating with the scheme to ensure that they have a skilled workforce in the future.

The training procedure
Make your first call the local Jobcentre. (Alternatively, you can ring freefone 0800 246000.) Ask for a preliminary interview to discuss ET. The officer will want to know about your background and education. You can explain your ideas about training and retraining.

You will probably be referred to either an Adult Guidance Agency or an independent local training agent. This will give you the opportunity to go into greater detail about the career you wish to follow. Alternatively, you may have an out-dated skill and require a course to enable you to readjust.

171

The training agent will discuss your skills and aptitudes with you, and offer guidance on the practicality of taking up training for the vocation you have in mind. The interviewer must then prepare and agree with you your personal action plan. The training agent should also offer assessment and plan your training needs. This could include complete retraining, updating old skills, or pre-vocational training. It will indicate the training which he or she thinks will suit you best, and the qualifications you should be able to acquire at the end of the training period.

The training agent, who knows what employment opportunities exist in your area, will then choose the appropriate training manager to implement your action plan. The next step will be to meet the training manager to organise your programme. The schedule will include off-the-job training at a local college or skillcentre, as well as a placement with a local employer. The general guidelines are for 60 per cent work experience and 40 per cent training. ET usually involves two days a week at the college or skillcentre and three days with an employer. In areas of high unemployment training managers may not be able to arrange an employment placement. In such cases they will offer project work as an alternative.

Job placement

Staff at colleges dealing with women returners with family commitments are understanding, so the hours spent at college or with an employer are often fixed to run from 9 am to 3 pm to accommodate school hours. Schedules can be rearranged with the help of a co-operative partner or grandparents. Many commitments can be met by late-night shopping and more efficient time management. (There may be opportunities for part-time training for those who have to be at home some time during the day because of family responsibilities.)

Some women may have to make a difficult decision. Should they take a routine unskilled job which produces immediate extra cash or should they undergo a period of training? In the long term, training should mean acquiring a new skill for a new job, or updating an old skill, coupled with the probability of a formal qualification as well as a record of achievement. The idea of job placement with an employer means that the trainee gets valuable practical experience (though unpaid), because the combination of work placement and training builds up earning potential. In some cases, when an employer has a mature person allocated to him for training, the willingness and ability of the trainee to make an effective work contribution merit a financial reward from the employer.

Apart from the job training, the two days spent at the college will also build up both the confidence of the trainee and the work ethic. There *must* be a commitment to the employer. No pressure will be put on the trainee to complete the course. The average time on a course for secretarial skills is between four and six months. Other courses may take up to 12 months. Monitoring officers normally report a gradual build-up of confidence as training and work placement proceed. The trainees themselves realise when they are ready and qualified to enter the job market.

Employers now take a more favourable view of the training programme. People on ET placement are not filling vacancies. Companies appreciate that women returners often have useful previous experience and bring with them organisational skills. The days spent at college may include courses in time/stress management and assertiveness training. Where no job is available at the end of the placement, another placement may be arranged while the trainee makes use of the Jobcentre and Jobclub facilities. There are often special facilities available for single parents. The college may develop work placements by telesales followed by presentations to local employers. Once placement and training have been agreed, the trainee's progress is checked in the placement company every six to eight weeks by the monitoring officer from the college.

Training courses

A typical college may conduct ET courses in bookkeeping and accounts, a business enterprise programme, carpentry and joinery, computer programming, hotel and catering work, job-seeking skills, hairdressing, beauty therapy, motor vehicle repair, nursery nursing, plumbing, printing and secretarial courses. In a country district, courses may be conducted in land-based industries including agriculture, horticulture, landscaping, machinery, countryside recreation and equestrian training. Foundation training is often available making provision for trainees of all abilities in pre-vocational subjects such as literacy, numeracy, communications and computer skills.

Included in the Employment Training programme is a comprehensive package for those thinking of running their own business entitled 'Enterprise Training'.

Case studies

Keith was 37 when he joined ET wishing to train as a motor vehicle mechanic. He had no previous relevant experience. He took up a placement in the service department of a large garage and has since made outstanding progress. He

173

has also been on day release for a City and Guilds certificate. He has now accepted a permanent post with the same company which has a firm commitment to a high level of quality training.

Janice joined ET to take a commercial update course, which consisted of six weeks' intensive college training and eight weeks' industrial practice. At the end of the 14 weeks, she took advantage of an additional course in word-processing and joined a maths workshop. She is now private secretary to a financial business management consultant.

John joined a Business Enterprise Programme course with the aim of starting and operating a small construction company specialising in designing and building plunge pools, saunas, etc. He completed both a plastering course and a brickwork course while he was in placement with a local company. He has now achieved his ambition of becoming self-employed.

Summary

A discussion with an Employment Training agent will enable your background history and skills to be discussed, your goals, objectives and aptitudes identified, and a realistic action plan agreed. The training manager, in turn, will be ideally placed to find you employment or suggest a suitable self-employment opportunity geared to the training you undertake.

The Enterprise Support Scheme (ESS)

The government is anxious to help people start up their own businesses successfully. Many unemployed people were reluctant to take the risk when to do so meant that they would cease to be eligible for unemployment benefit and income support. The Enterprise Support Scheme was launched to offset the risks for would-be entrepreneurs by paying participants in the scheme a taxable allowance up to £40 per week for one year. Currently, there are 90,000 places open to participants annually. Each local Training and Enterprise Council (funded by the government) can give you advice and guidance to help you get going.

The ESS is intended to help those who have received unemployment benefit for at least eight weeks, who wish to start a new business regarded as eligible for support from public funds, and who have at least £1000 to invest in the enterprise. (This may be arranged through a bank overdraft.) The business must be a new one. It is no good expecting public funds if you have been trading before you apply for acceptance into the scheme. Consult the Jobcentre before making any premature commitments. Ask if an Enterprise Awareness Day is to be organised. The scheme may be suggested to you at a Restart interview. After you have attended an Awareness Day, you may have to show that you are 'actively seeking work'. That is the time to discuss your plans with the Jobcentre.

After you start on the ESS you will be entitled to the weekly allowance in lieu of unemployment benefit and income support. An ESS team will check progress, give advice and encourage the use of counselling facilities. You can also use the facilities of your local enterprise agency and its business club. Ask the Jobcentre if you can try out your business idea under the Enterprise Rehearsal Scheme. You can also enquire about the availability of local business management courses under the Business Enterprise Programme (BEP).

If you are claiming Family Credit, Housing Benefit, etc and decide to enter the ESS, you will be walking into a legislative minefield involving several agencies. If you have any questions about benefits, there is a Social Security freeline confidential advice service. Ring 0800 666 555. This number is often busy. Ring in the evening, leave your name and number on the answer-phone and the DSS will ring you back the next day. This service is *not* linked to your local office. You can consult your local Citizens' Advice Bureau which will probably have a specialist adviser dealing with benefits. There may also be a local Welfare Rights Agency.

Recommended reading
A guide for unemployed people about using the ESS scheme to start up a business is *In With Your Eyes Open*. It costs £1.00 and is available from: The Unemployment Unit, 409 Brixton Road, London SW9 7DQ.

For detailed information on benefits the *National Welfare Benefits Handbook* is useful; it costs £5.50 from the Child Poverty Action Group, 1–5 Bath Street, London EC1V 9PY.

The local Social Security office, listed in the telephone directory under Social Security, can supply the free leaflet 'Which Benefits?'. Leaflets on Housing Benefit are available from your local council.

Chapter 8

The Job Search and Offer

You are now equipped to take the final, crucial step towards changing your career. You have considered yourself and arrived at a decision about the job type which best matches your strengths and has the potential for providing you with the greatest satisfaction. The outcome of that analysis could have resulted in any of the following four decisions being taken:

1. You identified a career for which you are already qualified.
2. You identified a career for which you need college training.
3. You identified a career for which companies can provide training.
4. You decided to become self-employed.

If your decision was 4. you should now read Chapter 9 where the possibilities of becoming self-employed are examined in depth. In this chapter we assume that your decision was either 1. or 3., so read on. If your decision highlighted a training need which could only be satisfied by a college course, this chapter will be more relevant either when you have completed the training or, better still, when you are close to finishing the course.

The job search

To be successful in your job search you must manage the undertaking as a project. You must plan it, considering each individual step clearly and in some detail. You must set yourself milestones to determine when each step should be completed. In this way the various aspects can be co-ordinated to achieve success.

But what is success? Overall success is undoubtedly measured, in the long term, by embarking on a satisfying career with just the right amount of future potential. The success of the job-search project in itself is quite a different matter.

Consider the following. With your second job offer you double your chance of obtaining the right job; with your third offer you treble it; with the fourth you quadruple it, and so on. Furthermore, if you can time the job offers to arrive simultaneously, not only do you have the advantage of choice, but you are in the strongest negotiating position possible with the employer who is offering you the job with the greatest appeal. More of this later, but at the moment you will appreciate that the job search objective is

Figure 8.1 *The job search project*

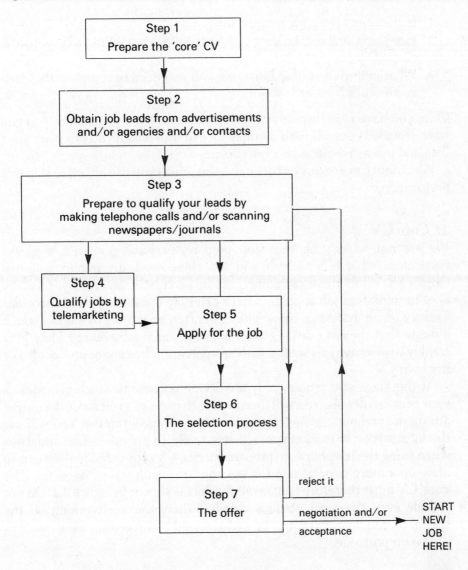

to time your project so that you are left with the widest choice at the job acceptance stage.

There are usually seven steps in the job search project. However, not every step will be appropriate for the job of your choice. Figure 8.1 shows a flowchart of these steps and we discuss each one in detail below. Your next task is to consider each step separately. Make notes in the margins and answer the following questions:

1. Is this step applicable to you? If so,
2. How long will it take you, including time allowed for a response, if needed?
3. What materials and/or assistance will you need to complete that step successfully?

Once you have read through each step and completed your notes, you will have provided yourself with a simple format into which you can place your data and produce your own project plan.

We cannot foresee any circumstances in which you can afford to skip this preparation.

1. Core CV

We are not advocating that you prepare, or have prepared, a glossy curriculum vitae (CV) which you can then hawk around to potential employers. While these can sometimes be successful, an employer usually likes to think that job applicants have carefully considered their particular vacancy on an individual basis. They can often be put off by signals which indicate that they are dealing with a 'professional job seeker'. They may frankly wonder what is wrong with an applicant who cannot produce his or her own CV.

At this stage you require only a working document which provides all your personal details. You will then be able to use it as a reference document during the preliminary stages of your job search programme. You will use this information to market yourself effectively, to provide details and dates when using the telephone, to prepare specific CVs for individual jobs, or to draw up a more general one for sending to consultants or agencies. The 'core' CV must therefore contain all the details shown in Figure 8.2. Do not exclude even the most obvious details. When you are working on the telephone you do not want to be embarrassed by forgetting basics such as your own postcode.

Figure 8.2 *Core CV*

Full name:

Address:

Postcode:

Date of birth:

Age:

Current employer/situation:

Current, or most recent, job title:

Length of service:

Time in current job:

Summary of experience:

Previous occupations, titles and dates only (reverse order):

Education/qualifications:

Specialist skills (languages, computing, etc):

Area of interest (job or training):

2. Leads

The job search project is, not surprisingly, a self-marketing exercise. Therefore, it should be conducted as a professional salesperson would manage the sale of a costly and complex product, a computer installation for example. To be successful you have to 'know your product' and prepare well, obtaining sales leads and learning about the client by identifying his or her needs before attempting to sell the product. A computer is rarely sold only in computing terms, but rather in terms of a solution to the customer's needs and problems. In other words, the client's attention is focused on the potential savings which can be achieved, rather than on the cost of the installation itself. Your case is very similar. You know your product – yourself – better than anyone else, but you now need to treat yourself as a 'product' by first finding your 'customers' and then selling yourself as the solution to their problems. Each of your customer's problems and needs will be slightly different.

This particular step in your 'sales programme' is therefore devoted to finding a number of potential customers. The more you find, the more you will be able to convert into 'offers to purchase'. There are three main sources of leads towards companies which may be in need of your services. We will deal with each in turn. You will need to concentrate on some or all of these methods to obtain the requisite number of leads. The number of leads you need will inevitably depend on the type of occupation you are interested in.

If you are making a major change in career you will, to some extent, be moving into unknown territory. The process of obtaining a job will therefore include an element of education. You will undoubtedly do better at your fourth and fifth interview than at the first. If this is the case, you will probably need to aim for about ten interviews because you want to obtain a number of job offers. With good application forms or prepared CVs, fully qualified candidates should be able to get themselves approximately ten interviews by applying for three times as many vacancies. This ratio is based on the private sector, where it is more likely that recruiters will only interview applicants who they consider have a good chance of success. In the public sector and the Health Service it is more likely that you will obtain interviews for a higher proportion of your applications. However, the number of offers made will be reduced by a similar amount. You now have to consider how many leads you have to obtain in order to find the desired number of interested companies or, in a salesperson's terminology, 'the qualified leads'.

Advertisements

These are undoubtedly the simplest and most straightforward source of leads. They are also, in part, qualified because they usually describe, in some detail, the job they have on offer and a specification of the type of individual sought. They do not usually tell you very much about the company or organisation they represent so there is still some work to do, but adverts are an excellent starting point. In some cases there may be sufficient vacancies on offer for you not to have to bother with any of the other sources of leads mentioned below.

At this stage it is only necessary to establish where you will find the advertisements that you want. The quickest way to accomplish this is to pay a visit to your local reference library, where you can see on which days the national newspapers advertise vacancies of the type you are seeking, which local newspapers are of interest, and which trade magazines are available. The more specific the publication, the more likely you are to obtain an interview as a result of your application. This is because the company or organisation is seeking applications only from people with some knowledge of the job. They will therefore pay closer attention to each application received than if they were inundated with applications as a result of a national press advertisement.

Agencies and others

Using employment agencies, consultants or employment bureaux can be both quick and effective as a good source of leads. However, there are some disadvantages of which you should be aware.

Obtain the names and addresses of agencies which you know have a good reputation, or which you have obtained from newspaper advertisements, or which any contacts of yours have used and can recommend. You will then have to prepare a generalised CV and a specific covering letter.

The advantage of agencies is that if they agree to recommend you to an organisation you may only be in competition with a few other applicants. Their biggest disadvantage is that they are in the business of selling individuals into jobs. Many receive no payment unless they place you successfully. One saying that can be heard in certain employment agencies is that 'There is a job of some sort for every sort.' The risk is that you may come under pressure to accept a job that is not ideal for you. Furthermore, anything said to you by an employment agency when they are 'recommending' a vacancy or offer of employment is not contractual. In other words,

181

nothing that the agency says to you is binding upon the employer. Most employment agency staff and some consultants have a selling background; they are not careers counsellors or personnel professionals.

These disadvantages are probably significantly reduced in the case of senior appointments where more experienced consultants or 'headhunters' are used. Such people often receive a basic fee irrespective of placement, so it is more in their interest to maintain a long-term relationship with the client company than to make a hasty appointment which could ruin that relationship.

Contacts

We all have far more contacts than we suspect. While this form of obtaining leads to possible employing companies involves the greatest amount of work in the early stage, any resultant interview will probably have the biggest chance of success as you may have less competition. At this stage, merely list everyone you know who may be able to give you advice or who may know of somebody, or some organisation, who may be worth talking to. A second list should be made of all the organisations (with their addresses and telephone numbers) who may employ people in the type of job you are seeking. Again, the best source is probably your local library, where you can be directed to such publications as *Key British Enterprises* which subdivides organisations into industry type for your convenience. You will then need to qualify these leads by telephoning individuals or companies. The final stage in the process will be to make further calls where necessary and to supply a specific CV or application form as requested.

3. Prep and papers

Prep

Prep refers to the preparation for the calls you will need to make in order to qualify the leads you have gathered from your lists of contacts and companies you have decided to get in touch with. It is crucial that any telephone call you make – being far more effective than a mailshot – achieves its objective. When telephoning friends or colleagues your call can be relatively informal, but it must cover a number of major points in a short space of time. In brief, you need to:

(a) make the person aware of the career decisions you have taken and the type of job or training you are therefore seeking, and

(b) ask whether he or she can give you any advice and help, or knows of anyone else or any companies you could contact.

We show a brief example of such a call in Figure 8.3.

Figure 8.3 *An example of a telephone call*

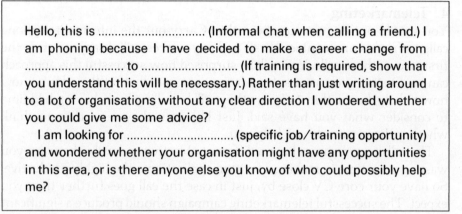

Hello, this is .... (Informal chat when calling a friend.) I am phoning because I have decided to make a career change from .... to .... (If training is required, show that you understand this will be necessary.) Rather than just writing around to a lot of organisations without any clear direction I wondered whether you could give me some advice?

I am looking for .... (specific job/training opportunity) and wondered whether your organisation might have any opportunities in this area, or is there anyone else you know of who could possibly help me?

NB: You should tailor the call according to how well you know the listener. It will sound very formal if used as a script.

Papers
During the preparation stage you can scan newspapers and trade magazines for appropriate advertisements. Do not lower your sights, but consider each advertisement creatively. For example, if you want to train as a physiotherapist and there is an advertisement for a fully qualified person in the location you require, why not telephone the physiotherapy department (not the personnel department) and explain that you have seen the advertisement, that you are not a fully qualified physiotherapist at the moment, but that you desperately want experience and training. Can they help or advise or give you the name of somebody else who could perhaps do so?

When responding to adverts it is important to follow whatever instructions you are given. If there are no instructions – simply an address, or the advertiser provides the option of telephoning before completing an application form – telephone. Prepare the content of your call and treat it as if you are qualifying this lead before wasting further time. The organisation will want to do the same, so have your core CV at hand. In general, if a company or organisation provides the option of taking telephone calls it is a good sign. It suggests that the company is particularly keen to recruit staff from the advertisement and that they are therefore prepared to take the trouble to answer the telephone and talk to people like you.

4. Telemarketing

You should not be nervous about this. Carry out the informal telephone calls to friends and contacts first, and any nerves will disappear after the first two or three calls. You will be surprised how successful this approach can be. On many occasions, friends may say initially that they don't know how to help, but within 24 hours they will be calling back, having had time to consider what you have said. Just like you, they need time to think whether their contacts can help you.

The calls to companies have a different objective and will either save you wasting your time in making a written application or be highly productive. So have your core CV close by, just in case the call goes further than you expect. The successful telemarketing campaign should produce a significant number of secondary calls in order to qualify new leads or to follow up promising ones.

Finally, this stage must include the preparation and despatch of follow-up letters where an immediate application has not been invited, but where a letter might just stimulate further thought or activity within the organisation. You may have to fall back on this type of approach if you are unable to contact your targeted individual. We do not recommend that you send the full CV unless you have been invited to do so. A good succinct letter will probably be more successful than a lengthy document in obtaining an interview. A draft letter is shown in Figure 8.4.

5. Applications

Your application for a job will take one of three forms:

(a) you will be asked to complete a company application form,
(b) you will be asked to forward your own CV to a company or agency/ consultant, or
(c) you will simply be asked for interview.

We will deal with each of these separately.

Figure 8.4 *Sample follow-up letter*

Option 1 (Where you successfully spoke to your 'target' individual, but were not invited to apply for a position.)

Dear ....

Thank you for your time and attention earlier today, when I telephoned to enquire about .... (your area of interest). Having had a successful career in .... (current job), I am now looking for a move into .... (occupational area of interest). My resolve to make this move has, if anything, been increased by what you told me today.

If there are any opportunities within your organisation that might be of interest, I would be very pleased to forward my CV or attend an interview at your convenience.

Yours sincerely

Option 2 (Where you have been unable to speak to the individual you targeted for your phone call.)

Dear ....

When I called .... (name of organisation) earlier today I asked who could provide me with some advice on .... (work area in which you have an interest) and was given your name. Unfortunately I was then unable to speak to you. Rather than continuing to trouble you by phone, I thought it might be more helpful if I wrote to you.

I am particularly interested in taking up .... (career and/or training details). I am currently .... (details of your situation) but, having carefully considered my future, now wish to make the move into .... (*If training is necessary:* While I appreciate that training will be necessary) I am very interested in joining .... (name of organisation) as a .... and would be glad if you could see me in order to discuss this possibility.

If you consider that there is someone else in the organisation to whom this enquiry could more appropriately be sent, please forward it on my behalf. In any event, may I contact you/your secretary on .... (state a date in five working days' time) to ask whether you are in a position to be of assistance?

Yours sincerely

The company application form

As soon as you receive the application form, take a photocopy. Most recruiters prefer to see a form completed in writing. Even when the vacancy is for someone with typing skills, recruiters usually prefer the forms to be completed by hand. This gives them a view of your written work and, in addition, application forms are never designed to make a typed response look well spaced and effective. Therefore, it is important to use the copy you have taken to draft your response.

Never replace an application form with a CV unless the company offers you that alternative. The reason for most application forms is to provide the organisation with a basis for your personal record if you are recruited and it is usually designed to provide the recipient with specific information in a standard format. When drafting your application form, complete all sections from your name down to your signature. You will find that, when you come to complete the actual form, the general layout will benefit from your being able to see the effect of bad spacing, etc. The golden rule in completing application forms is that you do not have to complete every available square inch of white space. Some application forms are not professionally typeset, so in order to fill, say, four sides of A4 paper before going to print, certain sections are simply expanded to fill the space available. While you should definitely answer every question, an attempt to fill all the space in answer to such questions as 'provide any further details you believe relevant to your application' is usually a waste of the reader's time.

Curriculum vitae

Here you are faced with the dilemma of balancing the importance of showing that you have prepared your CV on an individual basis with the workload this can involve. Anyone who has access to a word processor has a distinct advantage but, with clever design, you should be able to give each organisation the impression that you have prepared the document especially for them without having to retype all your details.

Your first attempt at preparing a final CV will often be the provision of a generalised document for an agency or consultant. This is a good start. Having developed the central pages with all your information shown effectively, you will only need to retype the front page, which indicates that it has been prepared specifically for that company, agency or consultancy. If you are in the fortunate position of applying for a specific post, rather than a job in an occupational area, you may be able to use the same CV for all the applications and merely continue to change the front sheet.

We have designed a draft layout for your CV as shown in Figure 8.5. You do not have to stick rigidly to the proposed layout, but the order in which you show your details is important. While your CV should contain all the information we have outlined previously, the order of each item must be tailored so that the recipient can read the most important and interesting details first; for example, whether the job applicant is aged over 25.

The details of your education are not the most exciting part of your history. They must be shown, of course, but not at the beginning of your CV. This message applies even where a university degree is a requirement – the organisation receiving your CV will give you the benefit of the doubt that you have the necessary qualifications while they read your application form. The important facts that the recruiting organisation will usually want to establish are your details, responsibilities and successes in recent work experience. This is why the best general approach is to have a brief introduction, as specifically oriented as possible, followed by a well-presented and easily read description of your recent career. It is also essential that your career details are not merely a list of job titles with companies and dates attached. Each job must have some narrative detailing the responsibilities and authority you have had, listing your successes and why you believe them to be such, and explaining how you benefited from holding that position.

Never criticise another company or a previous job even if you were let down or hated every minute of it. When applying for jobs, any hint of a negative attitude is easily interpreted in a far more general sense. This rule applies equally to interviews. A good interviewer can often relax you so much that your natural defences go down and you begin to talk openly about how awful a previous job has been. Never fall into that trap, because trap it is.

Returning to the layout of your CV, as the relevant information must be at the beginning, it is sometimes important to change the details of what is said according to which application you are completing. For example, you may always have held administrative positions, but are now applying for training to become either a probation officer or a social worker. In the former case, the emphasis must be placed on situations within each job where you have been in a position of authority over others and where you have managed to gain their trust and acceptance of your wishes, even though they were at first unwilling to co-operate.

Figure 8.5 *Curriculum vitae*

Page 1
Creating an Impact

This is the sheet which must convince an employer that it will be worthwhile finding out more about you so it is crucial that you create a good impression immediately.

State 'Curriculum Vitae' followed by your full name and address in the centre of the page.

Prominently, give a broad outline of your skills and the position you are seeking to take up. If it is appropriate you can also include reasons why you are making this application.

At the bottom of this page give a telephone number (including the STD code) where you can be contacted. If it is possible to give both a home and a work number, state both.

Page 2
Current (or Most Recent) Employment

The whole of this page should be devoted to outlining the details of your present, or most recent, job and the duties undertaken. Begin with the name and address of the company followed by a brief resumé of the organisation.

State the position held and in which department. Give the relevant start and finish dates, with any interim dates of promotion.

Explain the main purpose of the job followed by your main responsibilities and levels of authority. Give details of each activity in order of importance. Emphasise areas which you know will be of particular interest to a prospective employer. Stress areas of the job which have given you satisfaction or for which you received commendation.

Page 3
Previous Jobs

Working backwards from your present, or most recent, employment, give an account of each of your previous jobs. Supply dates and the position held, followed by an outline of the duties involved. Use a similar format to page 2, but be more brief.

Page 4
Personal Details

This is the biographical section, in which you provide information about yourself. Start with your date of birth and age. Give your marital status and, if you have children, state their ages. Next, list your qualifications and dates when they were acquired. If you are a foreign national, you should anticipate an employer's need for clarification of your eligibility to work in this country.

Move on to list your hobbies or interests. Include details of any clubs or teams to which you belong. Identify any positions of responsibility you hold.

You must now list the names and addresses of people who could be approached for a reference. Ideally one of these should be your present, or most recent, employer. State the position he or she holds within the organisation and a daytime telephone number. If your present employer is unaware of your job search, you should make it clear that this person must not be approached until a conditional job offer is made.

It is to your advantage to keep your referees informed of the job applications you have submitted so that they can be prepared to make a prompt response. Many employers prefer to use the telephone rather than write, so do forewarn your referees to ensure that they can give a 'spontaneous' but suitable reaction.

Salary

There has deliberately been no mention of salary. Keep this issue for discussion later.

An application for social work training requires a different emphasis. You need to stress how you had to exercise a counsellor's role, dealing with people problems of every nature. In fact, in such a situation you may decide not to put your job experience first. If your interest in social work or probation work has grown from activities unrelated to employment, you may wish to describe those first.

Remember that the exercise is still one of selling yourself. Your CV should give honest information. But recall that you are trying to address the organisation's needs and problems with your application. Therefore, you are showing, in an intelligent manner, your appreciation of the recruiters' needs by immediately bringing to their attention your strengths as applicable to their particular vacancy. Not only will they be grateful for this but their attention will be held by it, increasing the chances of your application being read fully and your being invited for interview.

Immediate interview

Do not just attend the interview. Without asking for it, the recruiting organisation will assume that, if you are interested in the vacancy, you will have prepared yourself and a CV for the job. You must therefore treat these situations in exactly the same way as if you had been asked for a CV. Do not send it in advance (good management practice but not good sales practice). Attend the interview and take two copies with you – obviously prepared for that particular company. At an appropriate stage during the meeting you can produce the CV. You can maximise the benefit of having prepared it by producing it only when the discussion has become so detailed that the recruiter is relieved to see the facts in black and white.

When preparing your project plan you must remember, at this stage, to include the time taken not only to prepare and send your CVs and application forms, but also the time you have to await a response. Our advice is to allow at least three weeks for a positive response. Some may take even longer, but your forecast can only be based upon the norm.

6. The selection process

To provide you with an introduction to this most important step we are returning briefly to our analogy between your selection process and the salesperson's task. By this time you will have worked carefully through the early stages of the selling process. You will have been able to identify some potential customers and have had the pleasure of successfully convincing one or more of them to set sufficient time aside to interview you, giving you the opportunity to 'close the sale'. At this point, it is most difficult for you to remain objective. You must continue to treat the exercise as a selling task and there are two 'rules' that any experienced salesperson could tell you about this stage of the selling process:

1. Prepare
2. Retain your integrity.

Strangely enough, it appears to be human nature that when it comes to selling yourself these obvious rules tend to be overlooked. Imagine that you were involved in selling a computer installation. It would almost always incorporate a maintenance service and guarantee worth a considerable fortune over a number of years. Once you had received the invitation to make a presentation to a customer, you and your team would probably work night and day to prepare for that meeting. Then, remembering that you are selling a long-term customer relationship, you would not suddenly begin to try to turn your computer hardware into a different machine. You would sell its advantages, you would have answers to 'cover' its weaknesses, but you would either sell it on its strengths or you would lose the sale to another computer with a package of strengths more appropriate to the customer's needs. You cannot modify the core of your computer any more than you can alter yourself.

In exactly the same way, when it comes to selling yourself, you need to prepare for that meeting and then sell your own strengths for all they are worth. Nobody is ever employed for their weaknesses (or even for the lack of them)! Staff are employed, and should be trained and developed for their strengths. It is these you must concentrate on and sell at your interview.

We will now consider these steps in a little more detail.

Preparation
This, in essence, is simple. Every ounce of information you can find out about your possible future employer will help you to get the job. Again, it is the reference library to which you must go. Librarians are usually librarians because they enjoy helping people to obtain and use information. In our experience the most effective approach is therefore to tell them why you are there and ask for their help. If you are applying for a job with a private company, you may need to buy a report on that company. For any organisation you must find out information and learn as much as possible

about them. In one form or other you will always be asked, 'What do you know about us?' You simply *must* have an answer, even if you begin with 'Well, I obviously took the trouble to try to find out a little about you from the library . . .'.

Good interviewers pay little attention to global statements, such as 'I thrive on stress'. They continuously search for examples of appropriate behaviour. Preparing well for the interview will therefore be taken as an example of all the following:

- Attention to detail
- Pro-active approach to work
- Commitment to your career change decision
- Ability to anticipate
- Intelligence.

Can anyone afford not to gain all these advantages at the expense of half a day at the local library?

Interview
There are many books written on the subject of interviewing and being interviewed. However, if you have prepared well for the interview there is little to be gained, and possibly much to be lost, by trying to bring into play any particular 'interview technique'. Remember our computer sale analogy: if you are selling yourself do just that – concentrate on selling, but do not try to change the computer. Interviewers, even untrained ones, want to be left with a feeling that they have gained some insight into their interviewee. Unless you are a professional actor/actress you will not succeed in giving them this impression about anyone except your own true self. They will only be left disappointed that they do not really know you well enough to make the decision whether or not they should employ you.

In addition to the above, however, it may be worth considering the following points:

(a) Dress for the part. It is not coincidence that all IBM salesmen wear dark suits and plain white shirts! Consider your audience and dress appropriately.
(b) Remember that an interview is a two-way process. The interviewer may well be a lot younger than you and painfully aware of the fact. One of your authors has managed capable young staff who have lost sleep and felt scared before beginning a session of important

interviews. If you can remember this and help the interviewer to be relaxed (without becoming patronising) it can only help your cause.

(c) You are likely to be asked about your motives for a career change. The interviewer will probably be intrigued, but also a little suspicious about your reasons for change. Consider your response carefully. It must not demonstrate that you have been 'driven' to change through previous experience. This is too negative. Far better to suggest that, despite being relatively successful and content, you were not totally satisfied, and as you only live once . . . .

(d) Irrespective of your abilities, one of the main reasons for taking the trouble to interview candidates is to assess their potential for 'organisation fit'. Anticipating such questions as 'How well do you think you will be able to work with younger people?' is obvious, but it will not convince an interviewer without reinforcement. You should therefore realise that this is one of the major reasons for the interview. Try to judge before the interview what they will be looking for. Ask any questions in order to clarify what they are looking for – and reinforce it for all your worth.

(e) Last, anticipate questions about your strengths, because these will be followed by questions about your weaknesses. The worst answer is no answer at all. The questions about your strengths are usually easy – that is why they are asked first. However, if you cannot think of any weaknesses you are too easily categorised as being either complacent or shallow. Therefore, think of some – preferably humorous and totally irrelevant to the job you are applying for! The best weaknesses are those that might be a strength in the job you are seeking. Strengths and weaknesses are always present, but are only relevant according to the job being considered.

For example, you may have been criticised for being too much of a perfectionist when you worked as a warehouseman. You are now seeking a job as a computer programmer. What a wonderful 'weakness' to raise in an interview for a programmer.

7. The job offer

Decision time at last. If your timing is right and you have benefited from a sufficient dose of luck, you will reach this step with a number of possible job opportunities open at about the same time. A degree of courage and diplomacy is required. Obviously, do not accept any job immediately – even if you suspect that it will be your final choice. Be honest with all the organisations you are dealing with, but do not go so far as to blackmail them blatantly. You cannot expect any organisation to wait much longer than a fortnight for a definite answer once you have received their written offer. In this time you must try to obtain any other possible offers, while keeping all the organisations assured that you are interested in their offer.

When you have received all the offers, select the one you like the best, identify any shortcomings and enquire about them. You may find that some of the issues are more negotiable than you first thought. Then write and accept. Your contract with your new company starts, even before you actually join them, when they receive your acceptance.

Jobcentres

So far we have covered the independent approach in your job search. Let us now look at Jobcentres.

If you are unemployed, or are soon to be dismissed as a result of redundancy, go first to your local unemployment office. Anyone applying for unemployment benefit must be actively seeking work. If you are unemployed, your claim for benefit will start from the day you first approach the unemployment benefit office, where you will be seen by a counsellor. Social Security rates change each April. Ask for leaflet NI 196 which summarises the whole range of benefits. It also gives you the reference number of the separate leaflets for each particular benefit. The counsellor will arrange for you to see the new client officer at the Jobcentre. For those who remain unemployed for six months there is a special five-day restart course, and you can use the services of the local Jobclub. Each Jobclub provides free use of stationery, stamps, telephone, typewriter and photocopier to help with job applications and CVs.

Staff numbers in Employment Service offices are rigorously controlled so be prepared to have to wait and to co-operate with the appointments system. You will find, however, that generally the staff will do their best for you. You must keep in touch with the Jobcentre. As new jobs come in, cards for each vacancy are posted up on the walls. Reference books and employers' brochures are also available. Useful publications available include: 'Get that Job'; 'Be Your Own Boss'; 'Getting Back to Work' (for women returning to work and those losing their jobs through redundancy), and 'Some Hints on Finding a Job'.

If you have firm ideas about your future career, the Jobcentre personnel will take this as a definite reference point and use their computer facilities in the job search.

Use the Jobcentre as a 'gateway' for all employment and training queries. The staff there have local knowledge and contacts. For example, a client who had been dismissed was seeking help to take his case to an industrial tribunal. He was referred to the Citizens' Advice Bureau who arranged a free 20-minute interview with a local solicitor.

Registered disabled people can ask to see a disabled resettlement officer. Jobcentre personnel are conversant with the 1944 Disabled Persons (Employment) Act which places a duty on certain employers to engage a quota of disabled people.

Jobcentres are now breaking down the old snobbish attitude that employers would not refer professional and managerial vacancies to the Jobcentres. Many employers now refer their job vacancies to the Jobcentres, which are in competition with commercial employment agencies. (The latter, of course, charge employers a fee for their services.) However, it is highly inadvisable to rely entirely on the Jobcentres when embarking on your job search project.

Armed Forces resettlement

The end of the Cold War was followed by a review of British Armed Forces. Cuts were planned to reduce the number of regular servicemen and women by nearly 60,000. In addition, some 45,000 civilian jobs were scheduled to go. The Gulf conflict complicated matters but, nevertheless, the regular forces will still be slimmed down considerably over the next five to seven years.

The three services have a well-established and efficient resettlement service programme. Having discussed the Army's procedure with Major P B Dixon in Aldershot, we urge members of the forces to take full advantage of the free advice and resettlement training courses offered before the discharge date. We hope this book will help to identify some of the options available so that as much preparation and training as possible can be completed in readiness for 'civvy street'.

For example, the army lorry driver is encouraged to use some of his leave entitlement to take up HGV assignments through commercial agencies. This brings home to the experienced army driver the cost-effective needs of transport companies, involving tachometers and the way in which goods for delivery must be loaded for safe transportation.

195

Housing is a pressing problem for discharged personnel as the sale of council houses has reduced the supply dramatically. There is nothing to be lost by registering on a council housing list years before discharge date. Any links with the area chosen should be stressed.

Those who have already left the services are reminded that the facilities of the 40 branches of the Regular Forces Employment Association always remain open to them. The Head Office is at 25 Bloomsbury Square, London WC1A 2LN; 071-637 3918. Ex-regular members of the Armed Forces who are unemployed are eligible for Employment Training (see pages 171–4).

Case study

When Peter left school, he joined the Royal Navy to train as an artificer. Recruits were trained to become supervisors, with naval discipline instilled. After two years' academic and technical training, he qualified as an aircraft mechanic. Having gained practical experience and promotion, he was sent on an advanced engineering course. He also gained an Ordinary National Certificate (ONC) in a recognised trade. Satisfying work followed on the aircraft carrier, *Ark Royal*, equipped with a Phantom squadron and helicopters. Fourteen years after joining the Navy, when he had been a Chief Petty Officer for six years, family circumstances forced him to resign.

During his period of notice, he consulted the Resettlement/Training Officer. Peter elected to go on a course leading to the NEBSS (National Examination Board in Supervisory Studies) at a technical college. This intensive full-time course covers the syllabus which normally runs for two years in evening class. Subjects included economics, finance, cash flow, trade unions (a new field for servicemen!), communications and interviewing techniques. Peter had a job lined up in quality assurance for electronic equipment before he left the Navy. He spent the next six months adjusting from a structured existence to one of 'total chaos'. The company soon made him a project officer dealing with an export order for submarine sonar equipment. After another career move as a production manager, he is now a manager in a company specialising in electronic/computer installations. Here all the contracts are different and challenging and so, intellectually, he is not stuck in a rut.

Peter leads an active life outside his job, and is prominent in a group raising funds for charity. Certainly, if the majority of servicemen and women who enter the labour market in the next few years are of Peter's calibre, they should have few problems in readjusting successfully.

Chapter 9
Self-Employment

The largest growth in employment opportunities will occur in the service sector – tourism, catering and miscellaneous services. We assume that you have carried out your self-assessment and analysis of your experience, skills and qualifications, and the possibility of working for yourself intrigues you. Consult your partner and family and obtain firm assurances of support if you decide to start up a business. Try to ensure that your health will stand up to the demands of your new vocation. It will not be simply a question of taking sick leave from your employer if you are ill – your business and capital could be placed in jeopardy. You must consider too whether your new way of life will affect your children's education.

Many large companies are 'contracting out' certain services. Such action by major organisations, as they try to concentrate on their core activities, provides fresh opportunities for would-be entrepreneurs.

If the area in which you live lacks a particular service, and you think you can supply such a need, this can be your starting point. Perseverance will be required as knocks and shocks are bound to occur on the road to success.

Case studies

Mrs G, a former nurse, and her brother launched a cut-price coach trip business from a rat-infested garage. Capital was provided by her father's redundancy money. Today she is the managing director of the largest bus and coach company in Europe and exports buses to China and Malawi.

Mr T lost his job when the carpet company which employed him closed down. Together with his wife, he launched a carpet business with 'a van, a telephone and dedication'. Carpeting is not bought from the suppliers until the client has ordered it. Sales now run at £80,000 a year. Mr and Mrs T say they 'don't want to be enormous'.

Miss B liked making jewellery but she lacked commercial instincts so progress as an entrepreneur was slow. Eventually, a satisfied client supported her flair for designing with capital and financial expertise. She now has premises in Covent Garden, a staff of six and profits of £100,000 a year.

A number of expense account company executives are being lured from city

197

centre hotels to guest houses in quiet villages. The saving can be as much as £100 per night. A former policeman and his wife, Mr and Mrs W, run a successful guest house in Yorkshire. Mrs W says: 'Our guests enjoy the change from impersonal big hotels. We treat them as members of the family.' Mr W adds: 'We make sure our guests can phone from their rooms but they are even more enthusiastic about my wife's apple and blackcurrant pie.'

Small businesses

What type of person enters the small business arena? Colin Mitchison, a Midland Bank Enterprise Manager, told us that the ratio of men to women approaching the bank for advice is roughly 50:50. Most of those who apply are in their early 30s. We asked for a profile of today's self-employed woman. He said that, in general, women are more considerate, thoughtful, numerate and less profit-driven than the would-be male entrepreneurs. Women enjoy greater job satisfaction and seem more determined about the quality of service they can offer. But the female newcomer to business tends to undervalue herself and to invoice accordingly.

Running a successful business requires the capacity to establish good working relationships with your customers. Colin urges his own staff in the bank to discuss customers' aims and ambitions with them. This makes the bank employees' days more interesting. There is greater job satisfaction in dealing with personalities than in churning out rows of meaningless figures. The client, in turn, appreciates the personal touch so that both sides get 'added value' from the transactions.

Four practical, jargon-free booklets have been written for the Midland's Business Start Service. These cover the first steps in setting up a business, the business plan, and the monitoring and control of the business. The booklets encourage prospective business proprietors to assess their chances of success and evaluate their suitability to run a business. They also outline the bank's services and describe the advice available to new businesses. The services available from accountants, solicitors and the various business advisory agencies are detailed.

The business plan

To prepare a business plan you need to know:

- where you are now
- where you are going

- if you have the ability to get there
- how you are going to do it
- how much it will cost
- how much you will get out of it
- if it is all worthwhile.

The Midland booklet enables you to put down on paper all that information you have had buzzing around in your head. If you require financial help, you will need such a plan and a cash flow forecast to show your bank manager. Completion of the plan and the discussions it will involve with your partner will clarify your thinking. Once you have your loan, you will need to introduce monitoring and control procedures. These will enable you to check actual progress against the targets set. You can then take corrective action quickly, if necessary.

Colin pointed out the transition difficulties a person must face when changing from, say, being employed as a lorry driver to being the owner of a small transport company. The budding entrepreneur must be available around the clock. His portable phone may ring with a transport enquiry when he is playing darts at the local pub. Similarly, someone offering an outside catering service must be prepared to work unsocial hours. Invoices must be issued promptly, an accounting system set up and slow payers chased. A small business is particularly vulnerable. If you are registered for VAT, payments to the Customs and Excise Department must not be allowed to become overdue. (The turnover figure above which VAT registration is required is revised each April.) Entrepreneurs must work hard at acquiring new clients, deciding whether to advertise, and developing marketing skills. Prices must be correctly assessed (with the help of an accountant). Overheads must be calculated properly. Without fleecing anyone it is essential to charge realistically. Everyone has to make a profit to succeed. Contacts are invaluable, as being self-employed can be a lonely profession. The Chamber of Commerce and Trade, Enterprise Agencies' business clubs, and Rotary, all provide worthwhile opportunities to meet other business people.

The Midland Bank supplements its Business Start literature with an amusing but effective video entitled *Help for Small Businesses* which can be bought for £5 (including postage and packing) from your local Midland Bank Enterprise manager. The video features an inexperienced would-be entrepreneur who has not thought through the implications of starting a business. It emphasises how a business plan will provide an invaluable benchmark to monitor actual progress once the business is launched. There is a need to assess the state of the market, and compare the strengths of major competitors with your capabilities. The costs of premises must be carefully assessed, particularly in the light of the new system of rates for business premises. Only when your estimated revenue has been checked by an accountant against your costs can you assess potential profits. The video should be viewed by the entire family. It will ensure they all know what is involved in the crucial decision to start a business.

Local Enterprise Agencies

Over 300 Local Enterprise Agencies (LEAs) are established throughout the UK with specific objectives to assist small and expanding businesses. Wherever you live in the UK, one of the enterprise agencies should be within ten miles of your home.

The range of assistance they provide varies, but the core service of the agencies is the provision of information and advice.

If you can't find the local agency in your telephone directory, ask your bank, Citizens' Advice Bureau or the information desk in your local library.

If you are unsuccessful, you can contact Business in the Community (BITC) which works closely with the agencies as part of its role to promote corporate community involvement. The address is: Business in the Community, 227A City Road, London EC1V 1LX; 071-253 3716.

Its sister organisation in Scotland is Scottish Business in the Community at Romana House, 43 Station Road, Corstorphine, Edinburgh EH12 7AF; 031-334 9876.

The Welsh arm of BITC is Cymru BITC Wales at Second Floor, Arcade Chambers, Duke Street, Cardiff CF1 2BA; 0222 221711.

What an agency can do

Your local agency provides free confidential advice on all aspects of going into business including:

- Finance and borrowing
- Marketing and selling
- Setting up and naming
- Bookkeeping and tax
- Premises and employment
- Advertising and promotion

- Patents and copyright
- Equipment and computing.

Each agency is geared to respond to local needs. For example, one agency undertakes over 1000 counselling sessions each year either at one of their offices or on clients' premises. Agency staff have a wealth of experience and have normally undertaken formal counselling training. The agencies are very effective, but many people already running small businesses appear to be unaware of their services. They are expanding their core counselling work, and provide extra facilities such as letting work space for small 'start-up' businesses.

Agencies can help to research a business idea and put together a business plan. They can call on experts in specialist business fields, and provide introductions to professional people and banks.

Most clients seek an initial discussion with the agency on the commercial potential of the business they have in mind. Preferably, this meeting takes place outside the client's family and working environment. Approximately 50 per cent of clients realise that their bright ideas are unlikely to have a commercial future, and that their enthusiasm and money could be better expended in other ways. It is better for such people to be disappointed at the interview stage rather than lose their precious capital later on. Other clients are encouraged by positive advice: many return for further consultation.

An enquiry was received from a man who wanted funds to buy a launderette. Asked what experience he had and his reasons for considering such an enterprise, he replied simply, 'Well, there is one at the end of my road which is up for sale.' Further questions established that the enquirer had no business experience, no capital and no knowledge of why the existing business had failed. Location is certainly vital to any business serving the public but it is not the sole reason to justify a purchase. A prime need for many clients is advice on marketing. Will there be enough customers wanting to buy the product or service at a realistic price?

Self-help clubs

Many agencies organise local business clubs to raise the level of professionalism. The self-help club provides a forum where people with small businesses can meet in a relaxed atmosphere, discuss their common problems, make useful contacts and fire questions at guest speakers. Talks cover such subjects as business taxation, business training, finance and marketing, trading opportunities, the business's image and relationships with the local press. Running a new business can be engrossing and time-consuming but meeting customers is not enough. There is a need to mix with other self-employed people who, though running different businesses, face similar obstacles.

Business ideas

The agencies' clients have a wide range of business ideas. Almost one-third are keen to provide services such as aromatherapy, car valeting, window cleaning, printing, beauty therapy, secretarial services, insurance broking, debt recovery, market research and sign making. Next in popularity is retailing, with clients showing an interest in selling anything from cheese to vitreous enamel nameplates. Consultancy, building and decorating are also popular but, surprisingly, the catering category appeals to less than one in 20.

Business training courses

The core of agency activities lies in the counselling of those trying to set up in business or in the early stages of operating a business. In addition, most agencies provide business training courses. Such training includes business awareness workshops, business enterprise programmes, and a 'Start Your Own Business' course. The 'marriage bureau' concept of matching requirements of clients with opportunities for them is practised where appropriate.

Workshop starter units

Many agencies control workshop starter units. In one area, for example, the units are used for the following small businesses:

Antique furniture renovation	Picture framing
Computer services	T-shirt design/print
Dressmaking	Business consultancy
Photography	Export consultancy
Limousine service	Bookkeeping
Nursing agency	Security firm
Food preparation (four different types including meals on wheels)	Upholstery

Advice from an agency consultant

We asked Barry Walker, a consultant, to comment on the current situation.

He said that, a few years ago, the long-term unemployed were the main problem. Now more clients in the 35+ age group consult the agency and they fall equally into three categories:

1. Long-term unemployed, with no ambition and no money.
2. Unemployed who find it difficult to get another job. People in this category are encouraged to become self-employed, and to enjoy using the skills they have.
3. Employed, but unhappy in their work or anticipating redundancy. They often have a good business idea, within their range of skills, and are motivated by a real desire to succeed. They may have savings or a redundancy settlement.

Today, with high interest rates, the greatest problem is cash flow and money management. People who become self-employed, and who have been used to working with large, disciplined organisations, are often nervous about meeting official obligations such as VAT, DSS contributions, income tax, planning permission and licences.

Many have good business ideas and the skills to put them into practice. But they may lack selling skills, and have problems in making sales. Almost without exception, new businesses undercharge. People starting up in business mistakenly believe that price-cutting is the best method of getting an order. They underestimate the time needed for a job, and worry about charging for a change in specification and for additional work. They volunteer credit even though they are not given it themselves by their suppliers.

Finally, those who intend to become self-employed must become single-minded in the quest for success. Running your own business is *not* a soft option. It involves worry and a lot of hard thinking, and a total change in routine. It needs the full support of the owner's partner and family. They must know what they are doing and like doing it!

Case studies

Mr N was employed in the catering trade but was disillusioned with his prospects. He gave up his job, decided to modernise his house and then looked for a new career. While decorating, he realised there was a need for up-market bathroom vanitory units. He produced samples and launched into business on his own. He then realised there was more to running a business than turning out the units. He contacted the agency for advice in the preparation of cash flow forecasts, pricing, and in obtaining finance. He

203

attended the agency's 'Start Your Own Business' course which enabled him to identify his problems.

Mr N said: 'I now realise how confused I would have been if I had not attended the lectures. I had no previous business knowledge.' The new business was started in a small unit but soon had to move to larger premises. With his bank manager's help, Mr N bought a unit on an industrial estate, from where he now trades successfully and employs seven people.

A garage service manager resigned from his job and bought a second-hand ambulance. Together with his wife, he began to deliver sandwiches to office staff. The husband and wife team now have five vehicles, employ 15 staff and offer a successful and profitable outside catering business including delivery of cooked meals.

A cost accountant realised that his post would shortly be made redundant. He had always enjoyed DIY and now operates a painting and decorating company. He has never had to advertise and is fully booked for the next six months. His whole attitude to life has changed – he 'whistles while he works' and has a spring in his step! His wife wishes he had made the change 20 years ago.

Ms O started her career working as a shop assistant in London. She was interested in fashion, and attended the London College of Fashion part time. She then progressed to a local technical college where she passed City and Guilds in Creative Studies with flying colours. Later she worked for various designers including Bruce Oldfield. As designing was her forte, she set up a small business in her own home with help from the Enterprise Allowance Scheme. The business did not go well and she approached the local enterprise agency for advice. Her counsellor advised that a change to more up-market products would be beneficial. Since then Ms O has not looked back. Output is directed to well-known retailers and includes the individual design of brides' and bridesmaids' dresses. Her trading company now operates from a unit obtained with the assistance of a local Economic Development Service grant.

A bookkeeper working in a small company had few prospects and limited earnings. He resigned and was encouraged to offer his services to other small businesses. He now operates a profitable bookkeeping, VAT and stock system service, and employs two people.

A Doncaster firm of poultry processors renovated a local factory. The company now supplies fresh and frozen chickens to high street supermarkets and quality butchers. The company has already provided 110 badly needed job opportunities.

An overview of agency activities

Doncaster
The Doncaster enterprise agency (DonBAC) offers financial assistance up to £100,000 to new or expanding businesses in its area which qualify. These loans may be used for machinery, equipment, building conversions and refurbishments. Advice to local entrepreneurs has created 5000 new jobs. DonBAC's ability to provide both training and advice places it in a strong position to offer a quality service to small, new and growing businesses. Courses at their training centre include marketing, selling, advertising, bookkeeping, business planning, basic accounting and quality management. Many courses are free. Monitoring of clients provides a check on the quality of agency counselling.

Cardiff and Vale Enterprise
Cardiff and Vale Enterprise manages 150 small factory/workshop units on nine sites across Cardiff and the Vale of Glamorgan, achieving 95 per cent occupancy. It plays a major role in the regeneration of 2700 acres at Cardiff Bay and in counselling 300 firms facing relocation. Five hundred and sixty-five separate businesses receive training.

Entrust (Tyne and Wear)
Entrust (Tyne and Wear) is one of 14 'Gatekeeper' agencies employing specific innovation counsellors to help inventors to develop marketable ideas. Advice is given on patents, marketing and design plus help in building a prototype. A sponsor is providing £100,000 as initial funding.

Shropshire Enterprise Trust
Shropshire Enterprise Trust is equipped with computerised business databases to handle business enquiries over the phone and provide hard copy. It helped to promote the selection of Shropshire as a pilot area in the National Rural Project with the objective of improving the rural economic and social scene.

Derwent Industrial Development Agency
This agency has played a major role in the renascence of the manufacturing graveyard at Consett in the ten years since British Steel closed down. Two hundred new firms have been assisted by the development programme,

creating over 500 jobs – many on the reclaimed 800-acre site of the steelworks. Businesses introduced include microcomputing manufacture and advanced biotechnology.

Glasgow Opportunities
Glasgow Opportunities (GO) was one of the first Scottish Enterprise trusts. It ran a pilot scheme to combine in-depth counselling and training for Enterprise Allowance scheme applicants. It has now won a contract to continue this and to provide Enterprise Allowance Days. GO's own newspaper reaches 10,000 businesses and decision makers in Glasgow.

Bolton Business Ventures
Bolton Business Ventures has conducted enterprise training courses for the ethnic minorities, using bilingual trainers. Funding was obtained for an Asian and Afro-Caribbean Business Exhibition. A client company received grant assistance to manufacture plastic rain hoods for pushchairs. The company now has a turnover of £1.5 million.

Your start-up

You can set up a business on your own or buy an existing business. You can operate on your own as a sole trader, set up a partnership or form a company. If you are going into partnership with one or more partners, it is advisable to have a solicitor draw up a partnership deed. This must cover the provision of capital, the sharing of profits, and methods of resolving disputes. Forming a limited company requires consultation with your accountant in addition to your solicitor.

Accounting procedures
We asked Simon Burke of Arctic Life & Pensions what advice he would give to anyone setting up a new business. He replied: 'You should consult a properly qualified accountant, rather than a bookkeeper, to discuss the accounting procedures that should be followed and the merits of establishing a new business as a partnership or as a limited company. Establishing the right accountancy procedure at the outset is important, as it will, in part, determine the amount of tax a new business pays in the first two to three years. By speaking to an accountant at the outset, you will be given guidance on how to prepare interim accounts, thereby saving the accountant

additional chargeable time when preparing and auditing the final accounts each year.'

Premises

For any shop serving the public the three golden rules are location, location and location! You need a flow of pedestrians past your retail shop, but customers will often seek out other services in less obvious sites. Research is essential.

Insure the premises (including loss of profit) and your stock. Consulting an insurance broker will cost you nothing. Ask your local enterprise agency if there are any subsidised 'start-up' premises/workshops to be rented. The agency's contacts will shorten your search.

Research

Use the facilities of your local reference library to research your market – size, what to sell, selling price, rate of growth, profitability and competition.

Advice can also be obtained from your local Chamber of Commerce, Citizens' Advice Bureau and the Consumer and Trade Advice Service of your county council. Ask your Jobcentre for details of courses and workshops organised by your local Training and Enterprise Council.

Key points

1. Identify a source of self employment which will give you independence and satisfaction.
2. Take the free positive professional advice available from your local enterprise agency *before* launching/buying your business. Use their counselling services, training courses and business club.
3. Don't undercharge. Meet business commitments and deadlines.
4. Don't become too busy to monitor debtors.

Franchises

We have written about the independence and freedom which self-employment offers. Taking up a franchise can be looked on as a type of compromise. With a franchise you gain the independence similar to that enjoyed by the owner of a small business, yet you have your franchisor as a 'back-up'. The franchisor will give you advice and support, provide materials (where appropriate), and help you in selling and marketing the products. The franchisor licenses a franchisee to conduct a business within the framework of a clearly defined procedure and method. The franchisee (the purchaser and operator) benefits from the experience of the franchisor (the owner of the brand and the operating system) who allows the franchisee to exploit the reputation of a branded name.

Types of franchise

There are three types of franchise. The job/service franchise is where a service such as car tuning, office cleaning, carpet cleaning or drain clearance is offered. You have to buy the equipment, receive training and earn an income related to the hours you work. The second type is the property/ product franchise which is based on a restaurant or shop. Here you sell a product for which the franchisor has stimulated a demand. Examples include print shops, quick photographic developing shops and fast food outlets. The third category covers high investment franchises such as Holiday Inns. (It will probably not interest you unless you are a pools winner or Aunt Mabel has left you a million.)

Much of the advice given by enterprise agency counsellors to potential proprietors of small businesses applies to franchises. You will be extended, mentally and physically, but you will not be breaking new ground. You will be paying to operate an existing system which, though it will not guarantee you success, will reduce some problems. You must accept that you have to pay for the franchisor's reputation and expertise. You will need determination during the time it takes to generate a worthwhile income.

Making a choice

First, decide on the type of business you think will suit your needs. The scope is wide and the choice can be daunting. National newspapers carry advertisements, but exercise caution. Some of the so-called 'opportunities' are not for franchises – they may be agencies or distributorships. Read franchisors' literature carefully, visit trade exhibitions and look at franchisees' premises. Beware of 'brokers' who may charge as much as £250 for basic advice and research, and agents trying to sell franchises for a third party on commission. Get a first-hand impression of the size of the market and the strength of the opposition in the area selected.

Taking advice

When you have a shortlist of possibilities, take professional advice from your bank's franchise manager, your accountant and your solicitor. The 'Big Four' banks and the Royal Bank of Scotland have specialist franchise units. Barclays Bank, for example, have produced 'Guidelines for Franchisees'. This will help to evaluate your shortlist. The guidelines contain sample questions to put to the franchise companies. How long have they been in business? How many outlets does the company have? To what extent will they help with site selection? You will also need to know the failure rate of franchisees selected. The information provided by the franchisor can be checked by your accountant and your solicitor.

It is essential that you talk to existing franchisees (whom *you* choose) and spend time in these outlets to appreciate the day-to-day problems. You could offer your services to an existing franchise as a holiday/leave relief. The experience could prevent you from making a wrong decision. One lady worked as a 'temp' in seven different outlets before investing in her own successful franchise. Ask existing franchisees about the adequacy of training given by the franchisor. You must concentrate on the *management* aspects. Can anyone take over when you are sick or wish to take a holiday? You will have to comply with the rules of the franchisor – opening hours, the goods you can sell, the selling price and the colour scheme.

There will be inevitable delays in acquiring and equipping new premises. Do not give up your present employment until you have to.

The financial commitment

Calculate the amount of capital you have to invest. The bank will require a substantial financial commitment from you, and will take a long hard look at the viability of the enterprise. It will need to see your business plan for the first three years, showing estimated profit and loss, cash flow and balance sheets.

There are limits to the financial assistance from a bank. Loans can be from £1000 to £500,000. The repayment period can be up to 20 years. This depends on the length of the franchise contract and the amount borrowed. Insurance cover is always desirable. The actual franchise contract, covering your exclusive business area, renewal terms and performance requirements, needs the attention of a commercial lawyer, preferably with franchising experience. (The British Franchise Association has a list.)

Franchises are proven

Michael J Marks, the director of PDC Copyprint, says: The franchisee gets his know-how from the franchisor. Banks are happier to advance loans to franchisees rather than small business people as they regard franchises as more reliable. Normally, franchisees stay in business longer than the self-employed. After five years only 23 per cent of small businesses still operate under the same ownership. Nine out of ten franchisees are still in business after ten years.

The franchisee looks to the franchisor for technical support and his buying power. McDonalds, for example, can provide potatoes, seasonings and flavouring because they obtain bulk discounts.

The franchisee can go to seminars to meet other people in the same line of business to exchange ideas and seek help.

The franchisee's commitments

The franchisee has to pay a royalty. The first year he may pay very little. After three years he may have to send the franchisor £300 a week. The franchisee should stick to recommended sale prices, will be told what colour the shop must be, and is not allowed to diversify. The person running a print shop cannot do picture framing as a side line. There is a limitation to diversification but not to growth. The franchisor has a good reputation and he wants it kept up.

The franchisor's role

The service must be maintained to a high standard. The franchisor *selects* the franchisee. Michael Marks comments: 'To many applicants we simply say that we do not think they will do well in a print shop. We may divert them into another line. If we like each other, we conduct a viability study. We will look at a possible town and sum up the competition. The site must not be too expensive or in a side street. We will help to negotiate the lease and prepare a business plan for the bank. We help with the training of technical and sales staff, give advice about shop fittings and equipment, and suggest suitable suppliers. We help to interview staff but let the franchisee make the final choice. We arrange the business launch and help to get customers. The life of a franchise agreement is normally ten years. If things go wrong, we will say *where* they are going wrong. We know the market and we research the product. We will advise on advertising. There will be ongoing training as technical advances occur, and information packs are distributed regularly. We provide a "hot line" to deal with legal queries. All members of the British Franchise Association should provide these services. The printshop franchisee makes the decision whether to go to "Kall-Kwik", Prontaprint or to my company. The essential thing is that the franchisor must be able to get on with the franchisee.'

How a bank will finance a franchise

The franchise manager of the National Westminster Bank explained that if a franchise is well constructed, the bank will apply preferential criteria to the franchisee as against the self-employed person to reflect the greater chance of success.

A sample capital requirement of a franchisee is as follows:

	£
Franchise fees	5,000
Shop fitting	25,000
Equipment	20,000
Initial stocks	5,000
Working capital and incidentals	5,000
Total investment cost	£60,000

In this case you will need 'start-up' capital of £55,000 and working capital of £5000.

The loan

For an established and proven franchise the NatWest franchising service may:

1. Loan up to twice the applicant's own input of capital.
2. Arrange a loan at a fixed or variable rate of interest.
3. Take a more flexible attitude regarding security.
4. Not necessarily consider prior experience in the business essential.

Banks keep computerised central records regarding all franchises.
Finance can be arranged in various ways:

1. *Overdraft.* This is designed to meet working capital needs. Interest is linked to the bank base rate.
2. A *variable rate loan* which has a flexible repayment programme.
3. A *fixed rate loan* (a business development loan). In such a case you know in advance the cost of borrowing. This is currently between 15.5 per cent and 18.5 per cent. The commitment can be up to ten years in the

case of a franchise and 'holidays' may be available for the capital repayment. There is an element of gamble as far as interest rates are concerned.

As security, the bank may want a second charge on your property. If the bank values your house on a written down basis at (say) £80,000 and it has an outstanding mortgage of £20,000, £60,000 is available as security. Alternatively, the bank may be able to take security over items such as life policies and stocks and shares.

Case study

Mr T C said: 'I had resigned as an army officer and felt I didn't want, in civilian life, to work for another mammoth organisation. I was keen to work for myself and had to reconsider my qualifications in a new light.

'I looked at various franchise possibilities, read magazines and waded through brochures. I then embarked on a process of elimination. Having decided what really interested me, I wrote to franchisors asking them for details. I prepared a list of 'possibles', and went to see the franchisors on their own ground. I needed to decide whether it would be possible to form a good working relationship with the franchisor. This is critical because you are entering into a type of "marriage".

'I went to see some quick print franchisees. You have to be cautious. If you talk to staff in the actual shop, you can get the feel of the place. I knew the geographical area in which I wanted to operate, but I found it difficult to get the right premises in a high street area. I hadn't appreciated that often a premium of, say, £20,000 was required, apart from the lease. I found the search quite frustrating. Eventually I decided to take over an actual franchise that was up and going.

'By now money played a big part in my life. I was no longer thinking in "broad brushstrokes". You have to have the cash in your bank account at the end of the month. Only then do you really appreciate the term cash flow! You may be making a good profit but you need to be able to pay staff and suppliers on time. Make sure you have an overdraft facility. I needed to buy printing equipment, and by doing so through my franchisor I got a discount of 20 per cent. There are pitfalls; you will make mistakes and you will lose money on some jobs. Tailor the business to do what *you* want. I took over in August and went on a skiing holiday in February. Everything was delegated to the staff and they enjoyed the responsibility. Organise yourself so that you can get away from time to time. It is entirely up to you. There will be sleepless nights, but when you have problems, ring up the franchisor and take his advice.'

How to choose a franchise

The British Franchise Association offers an information pack for prospective franchisees. Their address is: Thames View, Newtown Road, Henley-on-Thames, Oxon RG9 1HG; 0491 578049/50.

Mr Brian Smart, the BFA Director, recommends 'When deciding whether a franchise is right for you, you must examine yourself critically. Then, and only then, can you make realistic judgements about a franchise that will suit you.' You need to be realistic about three aspects of yourself.

Health and commitment of you and your family

Franchising is no easy option. You will invest a lot of hard work, as well as your money, over long periods of time, often during unsocial hours. You will take your work home with you, and you may take your family to work with you. Either way the stresses and strains will be as much your family's as your own.

Your financial expectations

Your expectations by way of earnings are as important as the amount you will have to invest. If your income needs are £20,000 a year, do not choose a franchise which can only produce £15,000 a year. Although the failure rate in franchising is low, failures are still for the same old reasons – you take too much money out of the business too quickly. Here you must take as much responsibility as the franchisor for checking the financial projections. Be sure you know the basis for those projections; be sure they apply sensibly to the particular territory you are considering. Be sure you check them against the actual experience of existing franchisees. Do not base your investment on what you hope will happen. Base it on a realistic assessment, a conservative estimate, of what has happened and what could happen. If the difference between profit and loss is only a 1 per cent point on interest rates you are at risk, so leave your rose-tinted crystal ball at home.

Your personal qualities

You must also be realistic about the kinds of business that will suit you, and take time to find out, preferably from the horse's mouth, what franchisees in a particular business really do – not what you want to believe they do. Some people go for the first franchise they hear about where the franchisor is willing to take their cheque. Don't do this. You need time to find out the

213

facts, and you need to compare the realities of one proposition with the realities of another and to find the best match with your own strengths and weaknesses. All this will take time. You should be looking for a shortlist of as many as six opportunities, acquiring as much advice as you can from franchisors, franchisees, the British Franchise Association, your bank and other professional advisers, and from the accumulated wisdom of two decades and more in a growing number of books and other publications on franchising.

Looking realistically at your own worthiness for any one franchise proposition, you will inevitably discover that you cannot offer every bit of knowledge, experience and financial clout that would make you the ideal candidate. Do not worry. Nobody is perfect and if franchising is about anything it is about training people with no experience, for example of printing, to manage a printing business. You should see in any franchise proposition a well-organised training programme that will fill in the blanks you recognise in yourself.

In the end it all comes back to realism. Be realistic about what you want out of your own business and what you are prepared to put into it; about what the franchisor can put into you and what you need from the franchisor; about the individual business you are proposing to buy – its cost, its demands and its potential.

The British Franchise Association (BFA)

The BFA was formed by leading companies engaged in the distribution of goods and services through independent outlets under franchise and licensee agreements. The aims of the BFA include defining ethical franchising standards to help the public and potential investors to differentiate between sound business opportunities and suspect investments.

All BFA members have to conform to a stringent code of business practice and undergo a detailed accreditation procedure prior to acceptance as full members. Remember, however, that no organisation can guarantee the success of your investment in any franchise.

Key points – personal
1. Digest all the information obtained from the BFA. Consult your bank's franchise manager and local enterprise agency. Employ an independent accountant.

2. Make sure you can work with the franchisor. Visit the head office.
3. Talk to other franchisees of *your* choosing. Check the market for the product/service.
4. Discuss all the implications with your partner.
5. Think hard about whether you will enjoy the business.

Key points – legal
1. Go through the franchise agreement carefully with a solicitor who is experienced in franchising.
2. Check the franchisor's background carefully.
3. Check that you have the option to renew the franchise agreement.
4. Check the extent of the territory you are allocated.
5. Check that you are permitted to sell or assign the business.

Readers in Scotland should contact the Scottish Development Agency, 21–25 Bothwell Street, Glasgow G2 6NR.

Case study

Roger left school with an interest in cars and thoughts of becoming a motor mechanic. But the prospect of getting his hands dirty and the image of mechanics dressed in oily overalls, working in untidy garages was off-putting.

Instead he took a white-collar job. Later he became commercial manager in the company's head office. But he still felt unfulfilled and frustrated. His company had no cohesive career structure: there was no motivation or team spirit. The only thing he really enjoyed about his job was the company car, which he tended meticulously.

He discussed the problem with his wife. Together they examined various forms of self-employment. They considered some franchise opportunities and came upon a mobile engine tuning service. Roger was interviewed by the company. He was unaware at the time that most of the would-be franchisees were garage mechanics, who were not acceptable. The company was impressed by Roger's experience in customer relations, which is the key factor in the franchise. Most new clients come from the recommendations of satisfied customers. Roger's interest in cars was a good basis for the technical training the company gave him. He now enjoys his work; he is satisfied with the back-up he receives from the franchise and he is kept up to date with the latest technology.

The Rural Development Commission

The Rural Development Commission advises government on all matters concerning rural communities in England, and acts to further their development. Its prime aim is to stimulate job creation and the provision of essential services in the countryside. The Commission provides grants to the rural community councils and ACRE for their community development work.

Through its network of local offices, the Commission provides a wide range of help including expert advice on finance, management, product-ivity, marketing, premises, training, rural transport, rural tourism, village shops, or obtaining planning permission.

To be eligible for business advice and help, a company should normally have no more than 20 skilled employees and be located in a village or a small town of less than 10,000 population.

The Commission's successful booklet *Action for Rural Enterprise* spells out the assistance and resources available – premises, finance, people, market-ing, advice and training. It outlines the scope for various types of business – tourism and leisure pursuits, fish farming, village shops, forestry, service industries and organic farming.

The Commission's Productivity Centre offers a practical service to cut manufacturing costs in any business. Special-purpose machines have been built to meet firms' needs and have produced dramatic increases in productivity. Successes include a candle-dipping machine and jigs developed to produce turned wooden products for the tourist trade.

For further information please contact your local office or write to the Rural Development Commission, 141 Castle Street, Salisbury, Wilts SP1 3TP; 0722 336255; Fax 0722 332769. State your particular interest and ask for their informative leaflets.

The Enterprise Initiative

Someone in Whitehall loves the word enterprise. After the enterprise agencies and the Enterprise Support Scheme we have the Department of Trade and Industry's Enterprise Initiative.

The purpose of the Enterprise Initiative is to provide a comprehensive package of services to help enterprises of all kinds to grow. To date, over 30,000 businesses have sought the help of outside experts to increase their competitiveness and maximise their potential.

Many entrepreneurs reach a stage when they know they need outside expertise to help them to expand, but they don't know how to start.

Enterprise Initiative can help through their Consultancy Initiative. In this way, the entrepreneur can reach experts in the private sector – experts in marketing, business planning, financial and information systems, quality, design and manufacturing systems.

The DTI will pay up to two-thirds of the cost of such specialist help for projects lasting between five and 15 days (including the time taken to draw up terms of reference).

The first stage involves a visit from a counsellor to carry out a short business review. He or she will keep an eye open for untapped resources, inefficient work systems and unrealised potential. The counsellor will give you confidential advice and recommend one of the DTI's specialist contractors to team up with a consultant. You get the specialist with the right background for your firm. The specialist will define trading objectives for your firm and specify the skills and resources needed to achieve them – the staff, premises, equipment and finance.

We suggest that you first use the free advice of your local enterprise agency, but if you feel you have progressed beyond their capacity to help you, telephone Business Planning Initiative on 0800 500200.

Chapter 10
Pensions

Whatever your age or occupation, a pension should feature prominently in your personal financial planning arrangements to ensure an adequate income in retirement.

Each year, the proportion of workers to pensions is decreasing. State pensioners are not funded from their own previous National Insurance contributions but from National Insurance contributions and taxes paid by those working today. According to the Green Paper 'Reform of Social Security', in 1995 there will be 2.2 contributors to each pensioner. In 2035 there will be 1.6 contributors to each pensioner. In view of the ageing population, successive governments have encouraged both individuals and employers to accept some responsibility for providing additional private pensions to augment the State's arrangements.

When retirement comes, you may have accumulated various savings and arranged for insurance policies to mature. You have been able to pay off any mortgage on your home. Your future income will include your State retirement pension and any occupational or personal pensions.

The State retirement pension

This consists of the basic pension, the earnings related pension, and the graduated pension. At present, the pensionable age is 60 for a woman and 65 for a man. The basic pension is paid in full if you have achieved a 90 per cent contribution throughout your working life. It is revised each April. The State Earnings Related Pension Scheme (SERPS) was introduced in April 1976 as an additional pension for employees but not for those who are self-employed. However, some people have left SERPS ('contracted out') by joining another 'approved' pension scheme – occupational or personal.

Under SERPS you will receive a top-up pension equal to 20 per cent of your average earnings which fell within the lower and upper National Insurance contribution limits throughout your working life, with a minimum of 40 years to be taken into account. The pension also includes a 50 per cent widow's and widower's pension. Higher benefits apply to those reaching State retirement age before 6 April 1999.

If you paid National Insurance (NI) contributions between April 1961 and April 1975, you will receive a graduated pension supplement. Contain your excitement. The maximum payable is just over £5 per week. Additional benefits are payable for spouses who do not have a State retirement pension in their own right. Full details are contained in NP 46 'A Guide to Retirement Pensions', obtainable from the Department of Social Security.

Occupational pension schemes

There are basically two types of occupational schemes – the 'final salary' and the 'money purchase' scheme.

Fifty per cent of jobs offer a pension entitlement for full-time workers. Company pensions administrators are now required to provide more detailed information on the benefits available to the members of their occupational schemes. If your scheme is contracted out of SERPS you will only pay NI contributions at the 'contracted-out' rate. Although you will not benefit from SERPS, the benefits from 'final salary' occupational schemes must at least equal those which would have been available from SERPS.

You can no longer be made to join an employer's scheme as a condition of employment but not joining may exclude you from other benefits such as life assurance, private health care plan, etc.

Final salary scheme

Usually, benefits accrue at the rate of 1/60th or 1/80th of final salary for each year of pensionable service. Take care, for in some schemes the accrual rates can drop as low as 1/120th for each year's service. Pensionable or 'scheme' salary will often be less than your usual salary – excluding P11D benefits (perks), bonuses/commission payments and sometimes even guaranteed overtime payments. Often, up to one-third of an employee's total remuneration consists of such payments. The pension will therefore be reduced proportionately.

Money purchase scheme

Contributions paid by and on behalf of each employee are invested in individual accounts. The benefits received by each retiring member are those which can be purchased by the funds in the individual's account. If the scheme is also contracted out, that part of the fund which has been paid for by the NI contribution rebates has to provide benefits which are paid in a similar way to SERPS.

It is possible for a money purchase scheme to operate purely on the contracting-out rebate only. The benefits provided are unlikely to be any better than those obtained by an individual contracting out under a personal pension plan, and in a number of instances they will be worse.

Securing additional benefits for a member of an occupational pension scheme

Most occupational pension schemes allow members to make additional voluntary contributions (AVCs) to increase their pension. From October 1988 the government introduced the Free Standing Additional Voluntary Contribution Scheme (FSAVC) which allows the employee's additional contributions to be invested, subject to certain formulas, with any insurance company. The maximum contribution to an AVC or FSAVC is 15 per cent of UK taxable salary less any employee contribution amount already being paid to the main pension scheme.

Tax-free cash

Most pension arrangements allow a proportion of the pension to be exchanged for a tax-free cash sum at retirement. An occupational pension scheme usually allows up to two and a quarter times the maximum permissible annual pension to be taken as tax-free cash. Personal pension plans allow 25 per cent of the funds available at retirement age to be taken as tax-free cash. There are, however, additional Inland Revenue rules which may further restrict the maximum tax-free cash sum.

Changing jobs/occupations/employment status

If you change jobs, there are two main considerations. First, what action you should take regarding your existing pension arrangements, and second, what is to be done regarding future pension provision. This depends upon the nature of your existing pension plan, whether you have been self-employed or employed, whether in future you will be self-employed or employed and, if employed, the type of pension scheme offered by your new employer. If the new employer has an occupational pension scheme, obtain full details with your job offer. When leaving an employer's pension arrangement you may become involved in refunds of contribution which will be taxed. You may have obligations to your insurance company. You may be able to transfer the cash value of preserved benefit to a personal policy under your own control, but this should be done only if you are likely to receive a better pension, which is often the case, or if you wish to retire early.

Many disputes arise concerning transfer values offered to employees with only short periods of service.

The overall situation is extremely complicated. If you think your career path will involve you in frequent changes, you may be better off with a portable pension plan.

Key employees and directors can become members of executive pension plans, and directors controlling 20 per cent or more of a company's shares can even operate small self-administered schemes.

Self-employment

The self-employed person will be able to claim only the basic State retirement pension. The need for the entrepreneur to make adequate provision for his retirement is therefore critical as the basic State pension is a very frail support in retirement. Self-employed persons are so engrossed with running their businesses that they are often guilty of leaving it too late to build up an adequate retirement income. Under section 226 of the Finance Act, 1956, and the succeeding Income and Corporation Taxes Act, 1970, self-employed pension plans ceased to be available after June 1988 when they were superseded by personal pension plans. Those with existing policies are able to continue with them, and there can be advantages in doing so. Retirement benefits can be taken between 60 and 75 years of age.

Personal pension plans (PPPs)

These were introduced in 1988. Under PPP rules you can take the benefits between the ages of 50 and 75.

The maximum contribution is initially limited to 17.50 per cent of net relevant earnings. This percentage increases in five-year stages from the age of 35 onwards starting at 20 per cent, and allowing as much as 40 per cent of net relevant earnings to be contributed after attaining the age of 61. The PPP is also permitted to accept contributions direct from an employer, and *this is the first time that an employer has been able to contribute to a plan which is owned by the employee.* The maximum percentage that can be contributed to a PPP has to include both the employer's and the employee's combined contributions. Contributions can only be accepted in respect of the first £75,000 per annum of an employee's net relevant earnings. This figure is revised annually. There is no limit to the number of PPPs that an individual may hold as long as the maximum contribution figure is not exceeded.

Summary

If you are in any doubt regarding future pension provision, it is best to seek the advice of an independent financial adviser. Yellow Pages are often a useful source of names and addresses but do ensure that the firm is FIMBRA registered. FIMBRA is one of the trade governing bodies and only independent financial advisers can be members. You can always ring FIMBRA on 071-538 8860 to ensure that the registration of the adviser is currently valid. If the advisers are not FIMBRA registered, it usually means they are employed by a single insurance company and can therefore only offer advice regarding that company's products.

Regardless of what pension arrangements a new employer may offer, it is *not* possible for membership of an employer's pension scheme to be made compulsory. You do not have to join any scheme you do not like the look of or understand fully. Many people leave pension planning until relatively late in life and then are surprised to hear that they cannot afford the type of pension they would like to receive. Pensions, or the lack of them, are an important part of everyone's remuneration package and should not be overlooked.

Key points

If you have to make your own pension provision, it is worth remembering that a pension plan is usually the most tax efficient savings vehicle available because:

(a) you receive *tax relief* on all qualifying contributions at your highest rate of taxation;

(b) your contributions are invested in *tax exempt* funds, ie your profits are not taxed unlike, say, a building society account that deducts tax from the interest before it is paid to you;

(c) most pension plans allow you to take part of the policy proceeds as *tax-free cash* at retirement;

(d) most pension plans today are *very flexible*, allowing you to vary your contributions or even suspend them from time to time.

One thing we can be certain of is that having a very small income in retirement makes for a miserable time.

Index

224